BEFORE THE FLAMES

——— * ———

BEFORE THE FLAMES

STORY OF DAVID KORESH
AND THE
DAVIDIAN SEVENTH-DAY ADVENTISTS

A. ANTHONY HIBBERT Ph.D.

Seaburn

New York   Lagos   London   Thessaloniki

National distribution by major distributors
This book is also sold at special discount rate to religious groups, schools
and institutions. For further information, please write to: Seaburn Publishing,
PO Box 2085, L.I.C., NY 11102

Library of Congress Cataloging-in-Publication Data
*Before the Flames: Story of David Koresh and the Davidian Seventh-Day
Adventists*

ISBN   1-885778-11-2

Titles - 1. Branch Davidians And David Koresh 2. Prophet Without Honor
3. A Unique Heritage   4. When Men Shall Revile You
5. Building Mt. Carmel Center-Waco TX   6. Inside Mt Caamel Center
7. A Message Like None Other   8. A Knock-Out Blow
9. Can It Happen Again   10. Let The Whole World Know

10 9 8 7 6 5 4 3 2 1

Typesetting, CSO, New York
Cover, B.C. Graphics, New York

Acknowledgment

Thanks, Penny, for allowing God to use you. Special thanks to Bill Payne (Penny's husband) for assistance above and beyond the call of duty. Earleen DeGolyer-Brownlee for unlimited use of your computer, copier, and Fax Machine, many thanks.

Whitney Williams, you are a true minuteman. Thanks for the use of your computer at the eleventh-hour.

Introduction

Much of the good in this world goes unnoticed, or if noticed, it is often scoffed, misunderstood, brought into disrepute, or laid in the dust. But like precious metal, sooner or later, it is unearthed by someone...somewhere. At such times, it is shoved to the forefront, strip-searched under scrutiny of a cynical world. However, this scrutiny generally reveals its worth. We cannot truly know someone or something until it is tried; until it withstands the buffeting of time, chance, and circumstance. If it is good and right, though weathered and worn, it remains illustrious. If anything, it shines brighter. Ultimately it will have its desired effects. It cannot fail. It will be seen for what it is—truth.

This sentiment is the hope and heart of a small, misunderstood, and much maligned religious group whose beliefs and highest aspirations are the ignition and current of their very existence. They have battled fanaticism, disappointments, debacles, and misrepresentations; but their faith and some unseen hand, seem to have guided them through many turbulent seas.

Davidian Seventh-day Adventists were obscure until February 28, 1993 when Federal agents endeavored to serve warrant on the Branch Center in Elk, Texas, several miles outside of Waco. The world watched, stunned as four Federal agents and some Branch believers were killed in a storm of bullets. A 51-day-stand-off between Federal officers and the Branch group had begun. It ended tragically in fire and ashes for most occupants of the Branch headquarters; including many children. This one event led the world, Christian and non-Christian alike to ask, who are Davidian?

Seventh-day Adventists? Previously hidden, now thrust center stage, where did they come from?

News reports seemingly linked the roots of David Koresh and his Branch group to a movement within the Seventh-day Adventist Church. A movement born in the 1930's by a Bulgarian émigré, Victor T. Houteff—a man with a message—a controversial message known within Seventh-day Adventist circles as "The Shepherd's Rod."

The world's perception of Adventism, especially Davidianism, was that of a crazed religious zealot and his gullible disciples.

Koresh may have taught and claimed many things, but in all fairness he did not teach or understand "The Shepherd's Rod." The truth is that Koresh and his group were a strained counterfeit of orthodox Davidia without a clue to the real Davidian message. If Koresh had a clue, he obviously chose not to represent it.

The aim of this book is not to cudgel Koresh or the Branch group but to simply tell the real story of these Seventh-day Adventists who have become known as Davidians. It aims at the truth the public never heard about Davidian history, beliefs, and goals.

The world does not know that before the Branch group, before the devastating flames of April 19, 1993, there were the real Davidians—a very different sort from some of their avowed successors. Houtef's death touched-off fiascoes, disappointments, and a would-be line of prophetic claimants, vying for power. The first to set out on this ominous trail was Benjamin Roden. He paved a highway of fanaticism for self-seekers and exploiters, a thoroughfare on which traveled a young man who later styled himself the Messiah—the Lamb of God.

Much of the world does not know that neither Koresh nor his analogues were authentic Davidian representatives. Orthodox believers existed then, and now, bearing the original biblical expositions of Victor Houteff. "The Shepherd's Rod"—a unique, challenging message to both skeptics and believers. A message that, over fifty years ago, forecasted today's economic, political, and religious state.

In many respects, this book chronicles the work of Houteff and all true Davidians. Their message. Their faith. Their insistence that the Davidian movement is heaven's call to earth at its "eleventh-hour," seems bound to emerge again, impacting our collective future. Not with mortal weapons, as in the case of the Branch, but with what might be called a heavenly vision. Does this sound laughable, or preposterous? "Before the Flames" invites you on an excursion. It sets course for a bitter-sweet journey into the depths of an unpopular movement that began yesterday, before the flames. A movement that could inspire the world of tomorrow.

Chapter 1

The Branch Davidians And David Koresh

History will not let us forget, nor time erase the events of February 28, 1993. It all started when a hundred or more federal agents endeavored to issue a warrant on Branch Davidian Seventh-day Adventists at their headquarters, near Elk, Texas, a small community just outside of Waco. The ensuing fifty-one day stand-off which ended in raging fire and the death of, according to most reports, 80 persons including 17 children. ATF agents engaged in a fierce gun-battle with Branch believers. It soon became the most disastrous day in federal law enforcement history. Nearly twenty agents wounded, and of that number, four died. Some were shot as they dashed from their vehicle. Others were killed or injured from multiple gunshot wounds. Ricochets and shrapnels rained upon them by Branchites firing from windows, doors, rooftops, and the guard tower. One officer was struck in the shoulder by a bullet fired from the tower. He continued battle but was floored when another bullet penetrated his helmet. He died instantly. Another officer rolled off a roof, struck twice in his lower torso.

Numerous Branch believers were also killed or injured. One Branch Davidian, hit by ATF sharp-shooters, tumbled off a guard tower and fell into brush. Others died from an array of gunfire which tore through walls, ceilings, windows, doors. Some were shot in the shoulder, thighs, hands. Their leader, David Koresh, was shot in the side and in the hand. He lived fifty-one more days to stage the most infamous standoff in American history.

Who was David Koresh? How did he command headship of the Branch Davidian Seventh-day Adventists? How did he gain influence to lead Branch believers to such an end? This chapter will answer these and other questions related to the Branch group, and in a secondary sense, to any cult-like organization. The study of how the Branch Association was formed and sustained, is more than history. It is a revelation of how a cult develops. For all who wonder, or seek to understand how one person could thoroughly monopolize "group thinking." The author trusts that this chapter will aid you in your quest to understand this phenomenon. It is not the intention of this chapter to cover every aspect of Koresh, Branch Davidians, or the standoff. Each has been widely covered in the media. Rather, this chapter will delve into unfocused areas of the subject.

The story begins in many ways with the land itself. The Mt. Carmel Center of David Koresh, was not the Mt. Carmel Center of Victor Houteff. But it was the Mt. Carmel Center of his successors. It was not the same people, for Koresh came long after the fiasco of 1959 to 1962. It was not the same mind set. It was, however, the very same property that Mrs. Houteff purchased after her husband's death in 1955 the heart of the 1959 fiasco, where over a thousand Davidian members gathered to await the ushering in of God's kingdom.

By the time of Koresh's leadership, only 77 of the original 941 acres remained. Florence Houteff and the Council, in 1961 and 62, had sold the majority of it.

The remaining 77 acres were seized in a kind of adverse possession by the Branch group. It involved a long court battle with a contingent of original Davidians and the newly formed Branch Davidians. Led by a soft-spoken, charismatic swashbuckler named, Benjamin Roden, the Branch was looking for a place to establish their headquarters.

Ben Roden was born January 5, 1902, in Bearden Oklahoma—one of James Buchanan and Nattie Roden's six children. He spent his childhood on a farm, and after high school, attended Oklahoma Teachers College. Later he worked oil fields in both Oklahoma and Odessa, Texas. In February of 1937, he married Lois I. Roden, who would later play a prominent role in the Branch's sordid history.

Shortly after the birth of their first son, George Roden, they were introduced to Seventh-day Adventistism through a wedding present from Lois's mother, the book "Bible Readings for the home." Impressed by what they learned, they sought out a nearby Seventh-day Adventist congregation. Baptized in 1940, they joined the Kilgore, Texas, church. Roden's zeal and energy in sharing his faith soon became evident and paid off. Within a few years Roden was instrumental in raising another congregation in Odessa, Texas, not far from his home. He soon became head elder of that church and served for a number of years.

Unlike most Seventh-day Adventist, local church elders, the Rodens accepted "The Shepherd's Rod" message in 1946, a decision which heaped persecution upon them. In spite of ostracism and eventual excommunication, they proselytized their new found faith, much to the denomination's dismay. In 1953, Roden and family resided, for a time, at Old Mt. Carmel Center (the new was not built until after Houteff's death in 1955) and worked in the farm department.

The Davidian message exerted a powerful influence upon Ben Roden, but not for the better. With his smoldering, radical tendency it became an able tool to grasp power. The Rod's message called for peaceful revival and reformation within Adventism, a transformation of the soul, a change of theories, certain traditions and practices, a non-compulsory spiritual metamorphosis in the order of things. Roden overlooked the essence of Christianity and saw an uprising, instead—a coup d'etat. Adventism as a whole seemed revolutionary to the rest of Christendom. Now here was a group of Adventists who had even more challenging and dissimilar themes. Roden and associates became misguided. Their actions revealed a spirit different from that of basic Christianity. Houteff, himself, was greatly disturbed by their kind of devotion.

The Rodens did not hold influential positions at Mt. Carmel Center. However, they possessed an affinity for fanaticism and self-promotion. (1) Considering Houteff's view of those who politicized, this may have been the reason he did not appoint Roden a more prominent role in the Association. Houteff's comments on the subject of position-seeking is fascinating.

"Plainly, one who aspires to position simply for self-exaltation, especially when such an office holds out spiritual responsibilities as does a church office, such a one should not be given any consideration whatsoever. And if he already has any station of responsibility, he should be relieved of it, for such high-minded leaders are spiritually blind. . . Moreover, this class of leaders, dead to Christ and alive to themselves, as a rule love to parade, and even to exaggerate their religious deeds. . . . This class of men are naturally clever. . . . .Multitudes are still charmed by such so-called good men, and multitudes unquestionably accept their decisions as if they were God's decisions.

"Take for example Jesus Christ. . . .Instead of preaching Himself, though, He preached the Truth. . . . He simply spoke of Bible truth, and gave God, not Himself, the credit." (2)

Even some secular writers referred to Roden as a scholar. He possessed leadership qualities. He had the ability to influence minds, especially in biblical matters. But, while Houteff was alive, no would-be- prophet or leader dared promote his agenda. To the majority, it sooner or later became obvious that persons like Roden were looking for a following. No matter their scholarship, they could not challenge Houteff's sagacity and theological prowess. After all, he had secured their knowledge of the original, profound biblical themes. Doctrines that had appeared irrefutable and had caused scholars to muse. Themes that had stirred the Adventist denomination worldwide. Houteff had accomplished the impossible without formal training in theology or attending any college or university.

Roden would be the first to launch a successful new movement. Within weeks of Houteff's passing in February, 1955, Roden claimed the prophetic gift. (1) Capitalizing on the disappointment surrounding Victor Houteff's death, he professed to be "antitypical Elijah the Tishbite"-the modern-day counterpart of the ancient, biblical seer who performed great miracles. Who, in a showdown on the top of a hill known as Mt. Carmel, called fire down from heaven, slew hundreds of Baal-worshipping leaders. Who was later translated to heaven without experiencing death. Unlike Houteff, Roden proclaimed, he would never die. He would finish the work and lead the 144,000 into Palestine. (1)

Roden drastically altered "The Shepherd's Rod" message, adding and subtracting where he felt that it was outdated or contradicted his own thinking. He began keeping the Old Testament ceremonial feasts, a practice which many Christian teachers, including Houteff, had condemned. His most outstanding claim however, was that he was "The Branch". The "Branch" is an Old Testament, biblical expression for the Messiah. Christians believe this messiah was Jesus. For one to assert that he was the Branch or any manifestation of the Branch was a profession to be the Messiah—the Anointed One—Jesus, the Lamb of God.

In September, Roden sent two letters out to Florence Houteff, the Executive Council, and the Association's constituency, announcing his new status. (3) The Council apparently did not receive the second and only a carbon copy of the first. Thus, it did not have full knowledge of what was about to take place. (3) Whether this was deliberate or not we do not know. Nonetheless, on October 8, the Association's office received word that Roden had called a worldwide gathering of Davidians at Mt. Carmel Center. Scheduled for October 10, he planned to unveil his new doctrinal positions. He would travel with at least ten others to pose questions to the Council. If they rejected his message great catastrophe would befall the Center.(3) Some believed fire would come down from the sky and consume the camp. (1)

By 10:30 A.M. October 10, seven carloads of Roden sympathizers arrived for the meeting. The Council, of course, did not call a world meeting. Their reason? "Such a meeting would have been contrary to the Constitution and By-laws which required that a general meeting of Davidians be called by the Executive Council. . . in advance in two consecutive issues" of their official organ, "The Symbolic Code." (3)

Before Roden left the Center, he walked building to building, his hands stretched toward the sky, invoking Heaven's fiery wrath to fall upon the camp.

Prior to his leaving the campus, some Council members did meet with the Roden band for a while on October 10. However, a more formal meeting was scheduled two days later. A difference arose about the place of assembly. Roden wanted the meeting in Waco. The Council wanted it at Mt. Carmel Center. Apparently,

Roden was to return a call, responding to the Council's proposed meeting place. When Roden had not replied by October 13, the Council called him. He stated, "that he was restricted by his message and could not come on Mt. Carmel property". (3)

Thus, the Branch Davidian Seventh-day Adventists were born. Neither Roden nor his devotees knew then the prickly path upon which he led them. They did not realize they walked a course that steered some to gun battles, shame, and an ignominious death. Roden would not live to eat the fruit of the seeds he planted. He would pass into eternity in 1978, years before David Koresh.

Although Roden was versed in polemics, he was unable to convince the majority of Davidians to join his radical, iconoclastic group. However, he recruited one or two questionable persons of influence. Perhaps the most noted of Roden's followers was M.J. Bingham. Bingham had been disenfranchised by V.T. Houteff, founder of the original Davidians, for his immorality. He was a well-read, expert grammarian who had assisted Houteff in editing "Rod" publications. However, he did not stay long with Roden. Later, he too avowed the prophetic gift and formulated his own group, the Bashan Association.

Perry Dale Jones, of Yoder, Wyoming, was known by much of the press, particularly those who covered the disaster at Elk, Texas, February and April, 1993. Jones was taken into Koresh's inner circle. In 1984, Koresh married Jones' daughter, Rachel. Jones died in the raid of February 1993. His daughter and grandchildren died in the inferno that ended the fifty-one day siege.

Verlis Johnson, of Kermit, Texas, another early follower of Roden, like Bingham, laid claim to Heavenly illumination. He initiated one of the two Gilead Associations existing today.

In 1958, Roden, his wife and two sons, went to Israel to establish a settlement. The event did not go unnoticed. Ministry magazine, a Seventh-day Adventist publication, carried the story: "For the first time in the history of Zionist colonization, an organized Christian group has been granted official status in Israel as recognized immigrants and land settlers, with all the rights of material and moral aid involved. A Year and a half ago, five families of Seventh-day Adventists from the United States and Canada immigrated to Israel to till the land and build new homes". (4)

This too was another giant departure from the original Davidian message. Houteff believed and taught that there would one day be a Kingdom established in the Middle East. He was convinced, from his understanding of Scripture, that such a kingdom would arise around specific world events, such as, world war, famine, and wholly by miraculous means without human aid or human intervention. Houteff never claimed rights to kingship or royalty in this kingdom. Roden, on the otherhand, actively tried to establish this kingdom through emigration and settlement. (1) His attempts and teachings would eventually blaze a clear path for David Koresh to follow.

Roden claimed that God instructed him to build another temple prophesied in the Old Testament book of Ezekiel. He was even told where the temple was to be—in Jerusalem, but not on the old temple site—the so-called "dome of the rock." (4)(5) In September 1978, Roden, his son, George and his daughter, Carmen had a personal audience with President Jimmy Carter, appealing to him to help build this temple.(4)

Roden attracted those seeking something new, and exciting. All who looked for an icon, someone to lead them, a prophet, found fulfillment in Ben Roden. However, in the opinion of most Davidians, Roden was a self-seeking, aggrandizer. He looked for a following at the expense of the Bible, Adventism, and the Davidian message. In him, they saw nothing more than a religious conman, capitalizing on Houteff's death, preying upon the insecure and unwary.

After Roden's break with the original Davidians in 1955, he rearranged the Davidian message wholesale. Fundamental Davidians did not consider the Branch "Rod" adherents. They had only the name "Davidian" in common. In fact, Roden and Branchites declared on certain occasions that the "Rod is dead." By that they meant that Roden's new message was the present truth, the new path to God and his kingdom.

Once convinced of this, they did not need to understand the

Scriptures for themselves. They were not obliged to harmonize fundamental Christianity, historic Adventism, or the Davidian message with Roden's. Roden was the inspired agent. He would do that for them. He told them what he thought the Bible taught and they accepted it almost without question. No matter how unbiblical or illogical, his reasoning became their reasoning. Rules of biblical interpretation were scrapped. The Bible was not the central guide, but only the tool of a central figure. A text simply meant whatever Roden said it meant. In reality Roden became more important than Christ—the key figure of orthodox Christianity, yet all the while professing to serve Christ. Therefore, he could claim that he was the "Branch", the messiah. Thus could Koresh claim the same title, "the Lamb of God."

This whole concept of iconoclastic prophets was not only adopted by Roden, but by nearly all later leaders of Davidian splinter groups. Each claimed to be some sort of effigy. The vehicle that allowed this abuse was an abstraction referred to as "the living Spirit of Prophecy." A key to understanding cults. We will explore this idea further in subsequent chapters. However, suffice it to say, this clever tool roped many into these groups. Roden developed and mastered this idea. Others would borrow it for their own benefit. Note that neither the Adventist pioneers, nor Roden's predecessors claimed veneration. Miller, White, and Houteff, believed they were special messengers. Whether one agrees with Adventist theology or not, an unbiased and careful study of their work would show that they rarely if ever stated that they were prophets only messengers. Although sometimes inferred, but never denied, they shied away from it. They never desired adoration. Roden and his contemporaries, on the other hand, had no such scruples.   Having established his views, Roden needed a base of operations. Initially he operated from Odessa, Texas, where he lived. As mentioned earlier, he made an unprecedented move to establish a colony in Israel. While working on this lengthy project, in 1965, he seized an opportunity to acquire the remaining 77 acres of New Mt. Carmel Center.

After the 1959 to 1962 debacle, the property—homes, barn, and administration building, had fallen into disrepair. Weeds sprouted,

17

and paint peeled. The once neat, well organized campus had deteriorated fast. A few elderly Davidian couples rented homes and stayed on as quasi-caretakers.

The remaining property was still up for sale. Mrs. Houteff, her family, and other Davidian leaders had started new lives. The rest of Davidia had dispersed in all directions. Years later, the main stream would reorganize and grow.

While contemplating another trip to Israel, Roden alleged that God directed him in vision to return to Waco, Texas. (4) Rodan wanted the New Mt. Carmel Property. In April, 1965, Roden contacted Attorney, Tom Street, who had handled sale of the property, and made an offer. (6) Shortly before arriving in Waco, Roden made a down payment of $2,500. Later that year, he placed $25,000 in escrow. Ray Bell of the Waco News-Tribune, recorded Roden's reasons for the purchase. " He wants to purchase the property to carry out the original Davidian aim of establishing a rest home for the sick and elderly. He also said he plans a Peace Corps-like project to train people for work in other lands. " (6) Most Davidians suspected Roden did not have such selfless aspirations. They believed he wanted the property as a base for himself.

The sale was blocked by a civil suit, pending for months. The General Association of Davidian Seventh-day Adventists, Inc., chartered in 1965, had leveled the suit against the original organization which had dissolved in 1962. After the 1959 fiasco, the former Association appointed Tom Street as trustee and liquidator of its assets, including the 941 acre New Mt. Carmel Center. The suit was designed to stop liquidation of the last 77 acres.

Contention had arisen over "second tithe", a fund reserved for needy and elderly believers. Allegations concerning the funds' distribution and misappropriations flew because of the dissolution and continued sale of Association's assets. This newly chartered group wanted the 77 acres remanded into receivership.

Third and fourth parties, largely older believers, contended that the Council acted illegally when they elected to dissolve the Association and sell off its assets. They believed that the various factions should come together, form one group, and continue Victor Houteff's original work. The old organization asserted that the Council, led by Mrs. Houteff, acted legally and Attorney Street should be allowed to continue liquidation. (7) It took six different attorneys to present the cases, including Mr. Street.

A long battle ensued. Florence Houteff, who had since re-married and had become Florence Eakin, testified, exposing the inner workings of the Association and defending the Council's dissolution decision. The case sprawled across local papers and television news-casts for weeks. It scuddled in and out of the court for several years. Oddly enough, Roden, uninvolved in the suit, would end up the ben-eficiary. How?

The old organization won its case. The judge ordered Street to continue liquidation. However, Roden, his family, and others of the Branch group gradually worked their way into residence at the cam-pus and took control of its operation. Former residents either moved out or passed away. Meanwhile the case went to the Supreme Court. While other suitors gave up, the Rodens pressed on, determined to seize the property. They avowed rightful successorship of the original organization and, therefore, entitlement to the property. In June of 1968, the Texas Supreme court, 10th Court of Civil Appeals con-firmed the previous judgment calling for liquidation of assets. It dis-missed a petition by the Branch group of 17, residing on the property. The Court eventually served notice on at least fourteen of them. (8)

Undeterred, they would have the property by adverse pos-session. The Rodens refused to leave. Shear prowess and persis-tence of the squatters prevailed. They declared that as "second tithe payers," those who paid more than the customary ten percent of their income, they were entitled to remuneration. They accused some of the leaders of taking $170,000 in back wage adjustments, (9) and not recompensing second-tithers properly. Of course the Rodens and many of the Branch believers were among those eligible for ad-justments.

They finally forced an agreement. Second tithers could either accept 19 cents on the dollar and leave, or remain and invest more capital. Roden, quickly swept up a combination of funds from various persons, donations from Branch believers and others, to purchase the property. (8) According to reports, the Rodens received $32,000. Remaining funds evaporated into legal fees. (9) The property became undisputed headquarters for the Branch.

Having acquired New Mt. Carmel, the Rodens continued to proselytize and push for a settlement in Israel. Within eight years of their acquisition of the Elk property, in 1968, they boasted of owning companies in the US, England, Australia, and possibly South America. By this point, it was well known in Davidian circles that Roden had declared himself the modern "King David" who would rule in the glorious re-establishment of the kingdom of Israel. He boldly proclaimed that he would not die. (1) Many Branch believers had already moved to Israel anticipating fulfillment of this grand promise.

To further his goal, in the Spring of 1977, during the Jewish Passover, Roden and his son, George, traveled to Israel. (4) He even built an altar of twelve stones on the top of the Mt. of Olives. (4) He was determined to establish the long awaited biblical kingdom of glory. But like Mrs. Houteff and earlier leaders of the original Association, they ignored the conditions and time for fulfillment of this kingdom. If the Scriptures are to be understood literally, (except where obvious figures are employed) as Davidians believe, then the kingdom will be established by unquestionable, providential intervention. Not by ordinary settlement. Houteff had taught that the kingdom would be established in a time of a gigantic world war in the Middle East, (10) with judgment upon the church, (11) during world-wide economic collapse, and distress of every type. (12) Traditional Davidians knew Roden, like post-Houteff leaders, was doomed to failure.

One can see why orthodox Davidian believers spurned the Branch's position. Learning that Roden proclaimed himself the earthly monarch caused instantaneous rejection. The icy response to the Branch group as a whole by fundamentalist Davidians was largely because Roden adopted highly speculative, unbiblical positions. He entirely remodeled the faith, promoted himself as an icon, misrepresented the spirit and character of the "Rod." They felt that he had capitalized on White's and Houteff's work, picking and choosing what he pleased. None of this discouraged Roden.

On October 22, 1978, Benjamin Roden passed away. His plans to establish the kingdom in Israel faded. By the 1980's, nearly all believers returned to their native countries. However, Roden's legacy continued. During the closing months of his life, he authenticated his wife as his successor.

Lois Roden stated that she too had been given the gift of inspiration. She claimed that the Holy Spirit, considered by most Christians to be the third part of the Eternal God-head, was female. She further postulated that the Godhead was like a family unit—father, mother, and child. Thus, you had God the Father, God the Mother—The Holy Spirit, and God the Son—Jesus. She later declared herself the earthly channel and representative of the Holy Spirit. Being female, she fit the role. Clearly, like her husband she forged a form of deity, albeit, more subtle at first. Roden affirmed her by calling upon Branch believers to accept the new teaching. (4) He even carried his appeal to the General Conference Fall Council in Washington DC. (4) Four days after returning from the Council, Roden died.

The rise of Lois Roden to the headship of the Branch Davidian Seventh-day Adventists, was generally accepted, and peaceful. Her husband, their former leader, had plainly confirmed her calling. Her authority went unchallenged. However, two major events forever separated the Branch from its predecessors and sealed its fate. First, Lois Roden disseminated her teachings not only to Adventists, but she focused largely on the outside world. Second, the arrival of 21-year-old, ambitious convert, Vernon Howell.

Although not as charismatic as her husband, Lois Roden showed organizational skills. Her decision to open her message to the outside world afforded the Branch greater world exposure. Its less exclusive program attracted a wider audience, constituents unfettered by Adventist's theological restraints. She maintained some of traditional Adventism—Sabbath (Saturday) observance, the non-use of "unclean foods", alcohol, tobacco and non-medical drugs. Most

Branchites were vegetarians. Focusing, by and large, on the non-Adventist world posed a significant change.

The original message and organization called for a "revival and reformation" within the SDA denomination and generally confined its work therein. After sealing of the sanctified ministry, the 144,000, and purification of the church, the pure gospel would light the world. Roden virtually ignored this and other key elements of the original message. As the post-Houteff leaders of the original movement, and her husband had done, Lois Roden continued divergence from the archetype. With these radical changes she maintained the Adventist-Davidian lingo, used similar biblical references and commentaries from Ellen White and V.T. Houteff. Like a huge magnet, it drew mystery-seekers, the insecure, and the unwary. Most will admit that certain books of the Bible have a mystique. If someone could unravel the locked codes and messages, surely they must be what they claim to be.

A word here, a line there, were all used to convince potential converts. Hebrew and Greek studies added further props to the new positions. What was unsupported by Scripture or Adventist predecessors was conveniently overlooked, ignored. When contradictions surfaced questioners were normally told, "That's old", or "that's dead", or "what he wrote or she wrote is good, but, you need an updated message". Ben Roden has been quoted saying, "get off the old Rod, and come on to the living Branch". (1)

It simply meant that you needed a God-inspired interpreter to help you understand what the Bible or the forerunners wrote. That person was Roden. Most converts to the Branch were never fully exposed to traditional Adventism or the original message of "The Shepherd's Rod." Some had not had exposure to mainline Christianity. Revealing too much of the traditional message could have toppled their new organization. Potential converts eager to learn about mysterious books of Daniel, Revelation, Ezekiel, saw the Bible in light of the Branch perspective only. Most converts exhibited a nodding acquaintance with Adventist pioneers—Miller, White, or Houteff. They had little knowledge of these individuals' history, and a vague knowledge of their writings. Only bits and pieces were quoted to support the Branch's doctrines. This rickety connection to the foundation of their theology left them susceptible to whatever they were told.

Orthodox Davidian teachers or ministers would agree, presenting basic "Shepherd's Rod" to a modern-day Branch Davidian would constitute news to them. Thus the Branch drew all types and paved the way for the second change.

The second and most profound change came with the arrival of a brash, good-looking, young convert, Vernon Howell. Howell never knew of the original Davidian message. Although a professed Adventist, he was excommunicated for revolting against Adventist standards on appearance, diet, and doctrine. In short, he was considered rowdy, fanatical, and a bad influence. Some believed he hungered for power. (1) For a year and a half or so, he tried rock music. He played professionally, for a while, recorded a couple of songs. About spring of 1980, he drove to the New Mt. Carmel Center for a Feast of New Moon Service and listened to Lois Roden's sermon on the Holy Spirit.

Vernon Howell was born to Bobby and Bonnie Howell on August 17, 1959. His Father was a carpenter. Within two years Bobby left his wife for another woman. (13) Vernon was left with his maternal grandmother, Erline Clark. A few years later he was moved to the Dallas area to live with his mother and stepfather, Ray Haldeman.

Howell's early years are somewhat obscure, but according to friends and family, he was generally quiet, and sometimes aloof. Some reports say that he was sodomized by other boys, and was prone to masturbation. (14) At six-years-old, he found refuge under the wings of his paternal grandmother, Jean Holub, a Seventh-day Adventist. She told John Berry of Esquire Magazine, that she took Vernon to Sabbath (Saturday) services and this had a marked influence upon him. "'Vern immediately felt such a peace in the church'. He loved foreboding passages of Scripture, which, she said, 'he just kind of inhaled'". (14)

Vernon was considered capable, but dyslexic, spending his elementary school years often in special education classes. While a teenager, he moved to Garland, Texas, attended High School, but dropped out less than a year later. He returned to Dallas and attended the Seventh-day Adventist Dallas Junior Academy. Within weeks his poor scholarship compelled him to leave. He moved back to Garland, but never completed High School. He was considered well behaved. That changed with the advance of late adolescence.

By 1977, eighteen year old, Vernon, learned to play the guitar and became heavily involved in rock music. He also worked at mechanic shops and garages and did some landscaping and handyman work. In the same year he moved from Garland, Texas, to Tyler, a conservative east Texas town. He later joined the local Seventh-day Adventists congregation. However, his relationship with the small church would not last. Within two years, he was disfellowshipped. Vernon periodically traveled to Los Angeles, California, where he played in various clubs, trying to make it as a rocker. Esquire magazine even reported that he made numerous trips between Los Angeles and Tyler. He was married and divorced on one trip, became a Satan worshiper and hard-rock fanatic on another. After the last trip, Howell said that he had a mystical conversion in a Tyler graveyard. (14)

The pivotal point of meeting 61-year-old, Lois Roden set his sights and changed his life and the lives of others forever. Howell's mother introduced him to the Branch leader. He soon embraced the Branch dogmas and traveled with Roden to various locations recruiting and shoring up parishioners. By 1983 he was her personal chauffeur and regular bed companion. Rumors testified that they married.

One account came from John Seraphin, a Davidian Seventh-day Adventist minister from upstate New York, who had numerous, private, frank discussions with Lois Roden. While at the Super Dome Stadium in Louisiana, distributing religious literature to attendees of the 1985 General Conference Seventh-day Adventist World Session, he conducted several cordial interviews with her. Curious, Mr. Seraphin asked Roden various questions about her beliefs and personal relationship with Howell, who was then elsewhere at the Session, promoting his own ideas. Seraphin said that at one point, during their conversations, he asked Roden if she was married to Howell.

She replied, "Yes." Somewhat astonished, the minister repeated the question. The Branch leader repeated her confirmation. "We had a good relationship", said Roden, "until he asked me to put his name on the bank account". She denied the request which severely strained their companionship. Whether that marriage was legalized or registered with the State is questionable. Stories circulated about her being pregnant and miscarrying. The two reportedly blamed the failed births on each other. (15)

The sour chord only created a permanent rift between them, but it purchased Howell the rancor of Roden's son, George. George viewed Vernon's apparent love affair with his 63-year-old mother, as a power play to control the Branch legacy and rob him of his future status.

Rivalry between Vernon Howell and George Roden began as early as 1983. George Roden accused Howell of raping his mother. Vernon tried to get rid of George, and George tried to get rid of Vernon. Bitter enmity towered between them. However, instead of loosing influence, Howell gained it. By 1984, Howell had acquired a following. He was viewed by some as a prophet. Perry Jones, a long standing, prominent Branch member, mentioned earlier as one of the first followers of Ben Roden, stated, "We accepted that Vernon Howell had a prophetic message. All of us except George, that is." (16) Howell's position was further boosted by his marriage to Jone's 14-year old daughter, Rachel, in 1984.

The battle between the two reached critical mass when a fire destroyed the $500,000 administration building and press. George accused Vernon of setting the fire. (16) Howell denied it. No matter. The possibility alone infuriated Roden. He drove Howell and his small band of devotees off the property at gun point, and termed the Branch camp, Rodenville. The ejected band, shortly thereafter, purchased 20 acres of wooded land near Palestine, Texas. They lived in abandoned school buses, lean-toos, and shacks with no electricity or running water. An unsettled Lois Roden exclaimed: "There are so many contenders for the Throne of David... seems anyone can become a prophet these days". (14)

Howell began visiting California, England, Australia, Hawaii, anywhere he could find potential followers. In 1985 he visited Israel and studied with several Rabbis. (17) February 28, 1993, he reported to FBI negotiators, in a KRLD Radio interview, that God instructed him to study and fulfill the seven seals of the New Testament Book of Revelation, often referred to as the Book of the Apocalypse. (17)

His efforts garnered more followers. Although not so charismatic in the beginning, the 25-year-old Howell became profoundly alluring. He played hard rock in clubs and strips looking for converts. He developed an ability to quote Scripture fluently and mastered convincing rhetoric. He was no longer the quiet, awkward, retiring boy who dropped out of High School.

One of his greatest passions was having multiple wives. He bedded Robyn Bunds, a pretty 17-year-old, California girl. He said that it was God's will, calling her his second wife. Later, he took other women as his wives, including Robyn's mother, who was still married and living with her husband, Donald Bunds.

Perhaps an equal or greater passion was his love of firearms. Howell began arming his group with various kinds of imposing weapons. He spent thousands on firearms and ammunition, all purchased legally.

He largely failed at reaching traditional Adventists, including orthodox Davidian Seventh-day Adventists. He convinced numerous Branch Davidians and non-Davidians. While the Rodens stepped away from Houteff's teachings, Howell ran away and closed the door behind him. Howell's new group scrapped all vestiges of "The Shepherd's Rod." Heavy metal music, playing in and attending clubs, long hair, smoking, drinking, sexual liaisons, and guns were never part of the original teachings. In fact, such practices were considered major taboos. They retained the Sabbath and believed in the re-establishment of the Davidic kingdom. Their only semblance. Otherwise the differences formed a Grand Canyon of disparity. These revolutionary changes attracted more proselytes than traditional Adventist-Davidian tenets' strict life-style restraints.

While Howell scoured for followers and grew stronger, matters at Branch headquarters, Rodenville, deteriorated. Lois Roden died in 1986. The entire campus was in disrepair and the organization was in debt. By 1987, rivalry between Roden and Howell escalated. Roden was a candidate for the United States Presidency, struggling to hold on to the remaining Branch constituency. With Howell's growing popularity, it was just a matter of time before he challenged him for headship. Roden prepared for the inevitable confrontation.

The challenge came in late 1987. Howell sent a letter and a notarized document, filed with the county clerk's office in Waco, labeling Roden a trespasser and asking residents of Rodenville to dispatch all monies to his group in Palestine. (18) Roden dug up the coffin of Anna Hughes, a former Branch member who had died years before, and challenged Howell to resurrect the corpse. Howell rejected the challenge. Roden, on the other hand, tried to resurrect the aged remains.

When Howell and his companions discovered that Roden had exhumed the body, they filed complaints against Roden for Corpse abuse. The Sheriff's department instructed them to get pictures of the body. They returned with a picture of a casket draped with an Israeli flag. They were told to get pictures of the actual bones. In the quiet hours of the morning of November 3, 1987, eight men, including Vernon Howell, Paul Fatta, David Michael Jones, and five others entered the property dressed in camouflage fatigues and armed with an arsenal of assault weapons. (19)

The results seemed inescapable—a gunfight. Roden was notified of the intruders and responded by clutching his Uzi semiautomatic. Within minutes Roden was locked in a heated shoot-out with Howell and his crew. Before long, the alerted sheriffs rounded up the warriors. Deputies seized 12 weapons, including a machine gun, 357 magnums, semiautomatic rifles, and large amounts of ammunition. (20) Surprisingly, no one was killed. Roden claimed self defense. Howell claimed they fired warning shots in an attempt to scare Roden off the property. (21) Roden sustained a hand wound and powder burns. (20) No one else was injured, unless you wish to include the bullet-

riddled tree that had protected Roden. (21) In Sheriff Harwell's words: "'They (Howell and his supporters) tore up a tree out there pretty good'. Mr. Roden had taken cover behind the tree. If they weren't shooting to kill, if it wasn't attempted murder well..." (21)
Roden's blunders cost him both the case and Rodenville. In court, he appeared mentally deranged. First, his charges were "vague and general", said Gary Coker, Roden's attorney. (22) Matters worsened during one of the court hearings at the McLennan County Court House. Anna Hughes' casket was hauled into the court room. Roden offered to resurrect the body, again. (23) To his further humiliation, the body did not even twitch. The Rodens, in 1968, had ignored a restraining order to leave the premises during the court dispute. When the court discovered this disobedience, it compromised Roden's case and kept him in Jail. (24) All eight of Howell's gang were tried for attempted murder. Seven were eventually acquitted. Howell's case ended in a hung jury and dropped charges.

Howell's takeover, however, was not yet complete. The Rodens neglected paying back taxes after acquiring the property in 1968. The debt stood well over $62,000. (24) Not even this stopped Howell. He and his group paid the taxes. What of Roden? Would he return? Roden was kept in jail for his injunction violation. He was also disciplined for filing an expletive-laden motion with the Texas Supreme Court petitioning God to inflict herpes and AIDS on the justices. The final cuff came in 1989. Roden murdered Dale Adair with an ax over an argument and was incarcerated in a mental institution. Branch Davidians took this as miraculous—heaven had spoken. God had chosen Howell. His takeover complete, Howell became the undisputed head of Branch Davidians.

With Roden removed, Howell restructured the Center. The disarray, clutter, and disorganization of his predecessor vanished, replaced by cleaner, more orderly facilities, strict organization. Residents arose early and worked long hours. They attended evening meetings where Howell preached marathon sermons. Everyone had particular responsibilities and had to carry them out. (1) Some residents worked outside the campus. Children attended public schools.

Although, they may have been withdrawn for long periods and taught at Mt. Carmel by trained teachers. (25)

It appeared that things were settling down at the Branch head-quarters. Branch believers were well known and generally respected by their neighbors. One local farmer quoted said, "If you're gonna write somnethin' bad about David, I don't want to talk to you." Howell was considered generous, peaceable, precise and well versed in the details of various trades, including farming. (14)

Neighbors could not see catastrophic changes occurring within the man and the camp. In May of 1990, Howell legally changed his name to David Koresh. David, has reference to ancient "King David", and Koresh is Hebrew for "Cyrus", the Persian king who conquered the great Chaldean kingdom of Babylon. This change presumed complete autocracy.

His claims, though, embraced more than royalty. He explicitly declared himself to be Christ, the Messiah—the Lamb of God. He established a new doctrine called "The House of David". By this he taught that it was his mission to establish an elite society of leaders and ministers for the soon-coming kingdom over which he was to rule. Members of this elite class must come from his seed. Thus, he was entitled to any female, single, or married. His followers were, not only to give him their time, money and labor, but also their sisters, friends, fiancees, and wives. Women chosen would become his wives and bear his children, joining the so-called House of David, located in California.

Rumor has it that he had more than ten wives— perhaps fif-teen. (26) Former Branch believer, Tony Kakouri, a resident of Lon-don, England, lived on the campus in 1991, and 1992. He reported Koresh saying, "that all women should desire to marry him and be his wife in the House of David. . .There was always a air of secrecy around the compound," continued Kakouri. "When new recruits were invited to the camp, children were hidden from view. Koresh had many chil-dren born to him from many different women on the compound, and it was kept very quiet."

Howell, now Koresh, became more and more radical, and

irrational in both teachings and actions. His lectures would "last about fourteen hours, some as long as twenty hours", says Kakouri. "The studies were conducted in a manner as to intimidate and brainwash the new comers. Koresh became very angry if anyone opposed what he was saying and also the same anger was visible and was directed at anyone who could not understand his conflicting doctrines." He became arbitrary, a law unto himself. One thing was acceptable one day, but not the next. They may be suddenly told to fast, or attend an impromptu lecture, eat only one type of food, or not mix certain kinds of other foods. While members were restricted from consuming certain foods, Kakouri observed that, "he smoked, drank beer, ate meat," when others were restricted to plain vegetarian fare. (1) At times he was very sociable, then he would become unexpectedly aggressive and disagreeable.

This Jekyll-Hyde behavior, self glorification and House of David doctrine, created detractors. Marc Breault, a disillusioned follower who left in 1989, convinced several disgruntled believers to join in an effort to dismantle the Branch group. They hired private detective, Geoffrey Hossack, and "signed affidavits alleging that Koresh was guilty of the statutory rape of two teenage girls, tax fraud, immigration violations, harboring weapons, child abuse, and exposing children to explicit talk about sex and violence". (17) However, their efforts failed.

Most of the constituency stayed, believing that Koresh was God-sent, the one to lead them to the kingdom of eternal glory. They clung to him as the instrument of all their hopes. They did not realize that he would not only demand their time, money, labors, and women, but even their lives. "David Koresh wanted people to die and kill for him". . . said Tony Kakouri. "He [Koresh] constantly said, if you can't kill for God you can't die for God." They did not realize that they would literally fulfill those words, and to do that, they needed guns.

Koresh was obsessed with power, sex and rock music. His fight for control of the Branch revealed his thirst for puissance. His House of David dogma revealed his hunger for sex. His all night playing sessions, at times not sleeping for days, (1) disclosed his craving for hard rock. His fixation with guns somehow edged out the rest. Perhaps, some may reason, that all stemmed from his former, power hunger. That can hardly be disputed. To Koresh, weapons appeared as the ultimate conveyance of might. How this craze for weaponry developed remains a mystery.

One thing was certain, he purchased guns legally, and lots of them. It has been reported that he thought little of spending over $14,000 for two dozen Colt AR-15 assault weapons, $1,300 for a Starlight infrared gun scope. (14) He or his defense crew, he called "mighty men", would frequent gun shows, and gun shops, buying up all sorts of advanced artillery. Some firearms were ordered by mail. It seemed that he was preparing for a confrontation with some well armed foe.

That he was preparing for some well armed enemy, is confirmed by several things. In 1992, he began a kind of metamorphosis of the campus. He built an armory. Members started target practice. Guard towers and look-outs were constructed. Enormous quantities of food were acquired and stored, some similar to rations used by US Army troops. He installed a thousand gallon propane tank, underground busses, tunnels, and hideaways. Koresh, himself, spoke often about the enemy—Babylon or the Philistines—understood to be the US Government. Kakouri revealed that "Koresh had it all planned to wage war on the USA (Babylon). The battle of Armageddon." In his Koresh's mind, this had some connection to the breaking of the seven seals of Revelation. This whole idea was so pervasive, that Branch believers nicknamed Mt. Carmel Center, "Ranch Apocalypse." Branch believers were convinced that a showdown was coming, and that at the end of the cataclysm they were to enter God's kingdom of peace.

In May of 1992, the United Parcel Service informed the McLennan County Sheriff's department that Branch Davidians had received deliveries of firearms exceeding $10,000. The sheriff's department contacted the ATF. An inquiry started which, by the end of the year, evolved into a full scale investigation. By February 25, 1993, the ATF Produced a "Probable Cause Affidavit in Support of Search

Warrant." A full scale raid plan materialized. The plan came into question. Officers discovered that the Waco Tribune-Herald had, for several months, been preparing an expose on the Branch groups' stockpiling weapons. They were about to publish their series, "The Sinful Messiah". The element of surprise was feared lost. If Branchites knew they were coming, it could spell disaster. In spite of that very present possibility, they issued the search warrant.

On the chilly, drizzly Sunday morning of February 28, 1993, 100, or more, armed ATF agents stormed Branch headquarters. Four federal agents and six Branch believers were killed that day. Among them was Peter Hipsman, who was a part of the 1987 shootout with Roden. Also cut down, was the 64-year-old Perry Jones, Koresh's father-in-law, who had started out with Ben Roden in 1955. At least five believers were outside of camp during the raid, including Paul Fatta, who was also a part of the gun-battle with Roden in 1987.

During the 51-day siege, approximately 34 people were released or left the camp of their own cognizance. Unable to convince the nearly 90 hold-outs, including numerous children, government agents tried to force them out with tear gas. Instead, the buildings caught on fire. In minutes, Mt. Carmel inhabitants were engulfed in flames. Nine escaped the inferno. The remainder perished in the fiery storm, including the man who avowed that he was the Messiah. Consumed along with him was his wife, Rachel, his 8-year-old son, Cyrus, and 6-year-old daughter, Star. Floyd Houtman, David Jones, and James Riddle, who were also involved with the 1987 shootout, perished with their leader. No one thought that it would end this way.

Although years have passed since that dreadful day, many unanswered questions linger. Who shot first? Did the ATF handle the raid appropriately? Did they start the fire? Or did Koresh sponsor a mass suicide? Is Koresh ultimately to blame for the disaster whether he started the fire or not? Is there a government cover-up? Questions and debate go on and on. A later chapter will briefly discuss responses to some of these questions. Answers may ellude us, but a fuller understanding of what took place before the flames may be reached. Perhaps then we will understand what to do after the flames to prevent another Branch-like inferno.

Some postulate that George Roden was the last Davidian. Far from it. Destruction of the Branch group was not the end of Davidia. The orthodox or fundamental line of Davidian Seventh-day Adventists traveled a very different route from that of the Branch. Many, of whom, still follow the original message brought by Victor Houteff. They operate several centers and facilities throughout the country. In fact, their numbers increase almost daily. They may have a profound effect upon society in the future. But nothing like the Branch group. How? This we will explore, later. Remember, no one thought, except Davidian SDAs, a little known band of Seventh-day Adventists, that their history would be splashed across the world's theater. But no one thought it would happen this way...Not this way.

Chapter 2

Prophet Without Honor

To truly understand Davidian Seventh-day Adventists and their struggles, one must burro into a mine laden with exceptional fortitude and a people of resilience. It is a narrative of the human spirit and that enigma of enigmas—faith. Fasten your seat belts; you are in for a ride.

Our journey begins in a hamlet called Raicovo, nestled in the Rhodope Mountains of southwestern Bulgaria. There, March 2, 1885, Victor Tasho Houteff was born. As Father and Mother Houteff cuddled that bundle of warmth, that newest family addition, they had no inkling of what the future held for their son. That someday he would shake a denomination from center to circumference. (1)

Growing up in a modest household, Victor certainly didn't suspect his destiny, nor did his three brothers—Nick, Leo, and Theodore, and three sisters—Anna, Marie, and Fimea. That his future held immigration to the United States where that unsuspecting denomination headquartered, was unknown to Victor as he explored the streets of Raicovo. That his brother, Nick would be the only sibling to follow him to the United States, was unknown to Victor as the two had played and shared secrets. (Nick would settle in Milwaukee, Wisconsin, and maintain a lifelong, close relationship with Victor.) However, these events waited many years and a continent away.

Victor had desired many things as a young man, but the two he had rhapsodized most were to know God and to be wealthy. That need to know God would become his consuming passion, changing his life forever. While living in Bulgaria, he had joined the Greek Orthodox church. There, he and others would be accused of conspiracy against the government.

The problem started when Victor and a cousin acquired their uncle's business selling roses. Sounds simple enough, right? Business had boomed, and they opened a shop in a nearby border town in

Turkey. Business soared. When Houteff's enterprise had begun exporting roses, blasting competition like a searing sandstorm, local dealers screamed, "Foul!" Knowing they piloted a fair and honest business, the Houteffs ignored all threats and covert attempts to ruin them.

Victor had learned, from the cradle up, to love God, be honest, work hard, persevere, and success would follow. Houteff's successful enterprise was a glimpse of his entrepreneurial skills—skills destined to become spiritual gifts as he grew in knowledge. A knowledge that would lead him to build Mt. Carmel Center, Waco, Texas, a training center for Biblical study, Biblical exposition, and publication of Biblical themes. Houteff would accomplish this on a shoestring during the 1930s as the US, and in some respects the world, reeled under the great depression. Built by volunteer labor, it would be sustained by members' free-will gifts. Its stately buildings would house up to 125 and grace a lush campus. Waco businessmen would be impressed favorably, unlike the businessmen in that Turkish border town. Houteff believed his success was owed to God.

In 1948 he stated, "when we moved our offices from California to Texas, where we had neither friend nor believer in the message, the church elders were glad, and thought our work would then die out for sure. It never the less grew more than before, although this took place in the midst of the depression, in 1935, while hundreds and thousands of businesses were going bankrupt, and while well-to-do men were becoming poor. Yet we who started out with nothing, grew and prospered. We, moreover, never took collections in any of our meetings anywhere and never made any calls for money. This holds good still. Then, too, our free literature that goes out week by week amounts to hundreds and thousands of dollars week after week, and year after year, besides the cost of building the institution." (3)

During earlier years in Bulgaria, Victor's future had glowed with promise. Partner in a thriving business at age twenty, his dreams of wealth had hung like ripe fruit ready for picking. Soon thundering threats from the opposition had destroyed all possibility of that fruitful harvest. The atmosphere toward him at church had grown cold. His fellow deacons and church brethren were also his bitterest competition. When they exhausted legal means of destroying the Houteffs' enterprises, violence erupted.

The prick of thorns on tender flesh while handling rose stems, Victor had known. The pain piercing his heart as he read the hate laced words scrawled across the front of his store, Victor had never known. The leathery weight of his Bible, during prayer and study, Victor had known. The weight of sorrow he felt when he held the brick that someone had flung through his store window, Victor had never known.

Chunks of glass crackled under their feet as Victor and his cousin surveyed the ravaged shop. They traced bullet holes in a wall opposite a window. The heavy perfume of roses filled their nostrils, rendering the scene as ludicrous as finding crystal goblets balanced on a trash heap. Who had done such a thing?

Many others depended upon the Houteffs' enterprises for their livelihoods, what would they do? How would they survive? Victor must have drawn himself up to every inch of his wiry, 5'3" frame. The roots of his thick, black hair might have bristled with Bulgarian indignation. Bearing his own suffering was one thing. Seeing the suffering of others was too much. This had to stop. Wasn't the rose market big enough for them all. Couldn't they compete peacefully; each dealer working hard to please his own customers?

Something must be done. Victor's faith in God, and his towering sense of right and wrong sent him into deep thought. He grappled with the need for justice, and decided to appeal to his fellow parishioners, the brethren he had grown to love and respect. They would surely reach a fair solution.

Imagine what degree of anguish must have assaulted Victor, as he listened to church prelates, and learned they had sided with his opposition on both sides of the border. How could they think that I had conspired to overthrow the government? He must have thought. How could they believe that I am an enemy of the state? Victor must have felt like a walking target for all their business woes. His membership in good standing, his dedication to God and to the work of the church meant nothing to them.

The bishop of the province, who had sponsored a campaign to discredit and ostracize Victor, turned to him with icy eyes and in a voice encrusted with cruelty axed all hope of justice. We don't know his exact words. Perhaps they were something like this:

"You're not welcome here. Your business isn't welcome here. Get out while you still can. Staying could be suicide."

Whatever the words, the danger was real. The church had a dead bolt on civil and religious power. Whether Victor realized the degree of personal danger is uncertain. Testimony shows he was incensed. (4) He felt compelled to denounce the church's hypocrisy regardless of who it was.

Few have the courage to stand by their convictions against the high tide of fear, abuse, or ostracism. Victor did. One respected, religious writer has said, "Of all persecution, the hardest to bear is variance in the home, the estrangement of dearest earthly friends." (5)

In most ways 1907 was like any other year, in other ways it wasn't. Couples married, babies were born, flowers bloomed, and one morning Victor may have realized he had sold his last rose. Fingers of fear must have clawed at his spine. Thoughts of his family and all the things he'd never do or see again no doubt crashed through his mind. He fled to his father's home where he sought security. The angry mob knew he would go there seeking safety. At gun point, they warned, threatened, and antagonized his family. Where could he escape their murderous mood? Sooner or later a bullet would end all of his hopes and his existence. More innocent people also faced harm because of him.

It was decided that Victor must leave the country. He must escape to America at once. His Brother Nick helped him secure passage, promising to follow as soon as possible (a promise he kept). He could stay with a cousin in a place called New York City. What a farewell it must have been. Perhaps Father Houteff gave Victor a solid squeeze, attempting to mask the fear that the family would never see him again.

Ellis Island and Lady Liberty with flaming torch greeted Victor and that boatload of immigrants. New sights, sounds, tastes, textures bombarded his senses. He navigated the entry process at a dizzying pace so different from the drone of life in Raicovo. How he missed his family and village. How he longed for a familiar face, voice, language, food. How would he survive? As he entered the streets of that bustling city, following the back of a cousin he barely knew, old hopes of someday being rich seemed far away and impossible.

Having survived the experience, he would later say, "Yes, hundreds and thousands of things may happen, but he that trusts in God and does his work well shall find all these so-called hindrances or mishaps wonderful deliverances, and avenues to success, all carrying out God's marvelous plans, and God's way toward your promotion from one great thing to another. When you are in God's care and in His control never say the Devil did this or that regardless what it be, for he can do nothing except he is allowed to do it. Always give God the credit.

"I came to America, not because I wanted to, but because God wanted me to. And since I knew not my future work, and as God could then no more make me understand than He could at first make Joseph understand his trip to Egypt, I was therefore driven out of the country at the point of a gun as was Moses driven out of Egypt, although I had done nothing to bring trouble upon myself. And who do you suppose led the rebels to storm me out of the country? None other but the Greek Orthodox bishop of the province! And where do you suppose he sponsored his pursuing campaign? In the church on Sunday morning while in his full regalia and about twenty feet from where I stood!"

"At that time I knew not what my going away from home to such a distant land was about, but now I know as well as Joseph knew that his brethren's hope to defeat God's plan for him was but God's plan to get him down into Egypt. And so rather than to thwart the plan, they really caused the plan to be carried out!" (4, 7, 8)

"Some years ago while in Europe," Victor wrote on another occasion, "I heard that one of my cousins had left for America. I then said to myself, 'Poor cousin, I will never leave home and go to live anywhere as far away as America for any reason.' But about that time, I along with others, was falsely accused of conspiracy. It was in the season when the nights were long, and as we put on the lights in our store one morning before daylight, a mob gathered with guns and stones, and stormed the windows. So it was that just a few months after I took pity on my poor cousin's estrangement from his homeland I found myself in America in the same house with him. It was a great disappointment at first, no not lesser than Joseph's of old, but what a favor at last! God bless the mob!" (9)

Thoughts of starvation and destitution disappeared as Victor hoisted pots and pans—fried, baked, sliced, and diced as assistant cook in a New York restaurant. Mom's home cooking it wasn't, but he had a job. His halting English flavored with a hefty Bulgarian brogue may have enhanced his credibility. Anyone who spoke like that had to be a European chef in waiting, a culinary genius. Whether he was or not, Victor appreciated that skill in others. He grew to understand the relationship between well prepared, wholesome food and good health. Years later he would say, "A ten talented person is a cook." After establishing Mount Carmel Center, he would make sure the cooks' wages, though sacrificial by secular standards, were among the highest. (4)

In that New York restaurant, Victor Houteff may have sounded like a famous European chef, but he looked like a schoolmaster. Piercing black eyes behind wire-rimmed glasses, slender 5'3" build, he usually wore suits in public. Gentle, quiet spoken, he possessed a distinctive laugh, and a generous love for children.

During his years at Mount Carmel Center, though well groomed in public, in casual or working moments, he often wore a rumpled, wool sweater and tattered shoes with a hole in the sole. When asked to change, he would smile but decidedly refuse.

Houteff's unassuming demeanor almost masked his scholarly sagacity. Even after mastering the English language, his notable brogue remained a strong indicator of his heritage. Upon reviewing Houteff's first book, one elder of the protestant denomination he later joined, critically suggested that he have the book "proof-read by an English teacher." The elder's objection was not over poor grammar but

Houteff's bluntness, lack of refinement.

Houteff's reply, "I believe you are sincere in this Elder_____, and I appreciate your admonition; but I also believe you will give earnest attention to what I am about to say, as I will try to explain my position in the fear of the Lord.

"As I said before, I have nothing in "The Shepherd's Rod" [the name of his book] to my knowledge that has no bearing on the 144,000 and a call for reformation. I think if you will study it from that angle, you will see that my statement is correct. This is one of the reasons why we did not leave out any of the topics. Our second reason is, the truth of the 144,000 came through these topics to which many have objected, and doubtless you perhaps refer to the same things. Now, Elder_____, stop and think how foolish it would be to kill the hen as soon as the chickens are hatched out!

"I agree with you, Elder_____, if I had my way I would never have written the idea the way it is. I would have put in all the nice things, and left out all the rebuff and condemnation. I would have hired the finest English teacher I could get and have him clothe the thing in good, flowery language; thus making sure that it would find a welcome in every home. But had I done so, it would have contradicted the very principle it stands for, and the tune of its voice would have condemned its profession. In other words, it would have been non-descript—"lamb-like," but speaking like a dragon." (10) Much more will be said about these doctrinal positions and the controversy they raised in Adventism.

For one who arrived on these shores not knowing the language, to master it without formal training better than many English students, was a formidable accomplishment. To write thousands of pages on Biblical exposition, having them published and distributed worldwide was remarkable. Houteff did have the assistance of Mr. H.G. Warden in writing his first volume of 255 pages and his second of 304 pages. Mr. M.J. Bingham, a linguist and grammarian, helped him in his later works.

His command of language was not the most outstanding feature of his writing. The concepts of theology that illumined the Bible in unimaginable ways was outstanding and powerful.

At this juncture though, he was still a Greek Orthodox believer, seeking a new life in a new world, reviving his dream of being wealthy. It was not to be. He was once again steered away from his material hopes. His brother, Nick, immigrated to the US, and settled down in Milwaukee. Victor decided to join him there.

In 1919, Houteff bought a small hotel in Rockford, Illinois. Prosperity beckoned. One night while traveling the streets of Rockford, he came upon a tent meeting sponsored by the Seventh-day Adventists. His intense interest in religion roused. He took a seat and listened to the speaker. He returned night after night and became thoroughly convinced of the truth of their teachings. He embraced their faith and joined their church.

Evidence suggests that church members stayed at his hotel, checking in early Friday, leaving early Sunday. Compelled by conviction, after becoming a Seventh-day Adventist, he would close the hotel on Sabbaths. (4) He was a faithful, conscientious believer, perhaps more dedicated to Adventism than he had been to Greek Orthodoxy. Convinced that this was the truth, he diligently supported the church and practiced his beliefs. It filled his hungry soul. He placed all in God's hands willing to do whatever it took to remain true to Him.

Regardless of the sacrifice Houteff cherished this experience. Christ was now real to him, and he believed that what he had accepted were the words of his Lord unfolded. His renouncing Eastern Orthodoxy and embracing Adventism marked another important event in his life. Like fleeing Bulgaria, it would lead him down a road of more life changes than he could imagine.

Although his desire to know God and His word was coming to full view, his hope of being wealthy was again fading. Instead, a life of poverty towered before him barricading all of his material plans. Confirming this vision of failure and poverty, church members themselves were poor. He observed, "They were at the time meeting in a rented hall, not too attractive for a church. The people appeared to be very poor. Aside from the preacher I was the only one that was driving a car, and he had a worn out Ford that I would not have given a dollar for it if I had to drive it.

"Imagine now," continues Houteff, "what went through my mind, and you may know that I joined the church only for truth's sake. Indeed, I had no other encouragement. My hopes of getting rich some-day became a nightmare of getting poorer. Yes, the devil gave me as good a picture of poverty as he gave the Lord a picture of the glory of the kingdoms. I nevertheless resolved to stay by the truth I had learned regardless what happened.

"The time came that I sold the hotel and accidentally got into a grocery business. After a time I found that I did not want to be in it, and I sold it at a loss. Then that dark and gloomy picture of coming poverty enlarged itself a hundred-fold, but I did my best to keep happy in the Lord." (7)

After disposing of the grocery store, Houteff left the city and six months later went to Los Angeles, California. However, life wouldn't get any easier. He fell extremely ill, and one of the retired church pastors referred him to the Glendale Sanitarium (now Glendale Hospital). In the 1920s it was operated by the church. Being an active member in good and regular standing, Houteff anticipated prime service and lower rates. He expected a church owned and operated facility to treat all patrons with love, courtesy, and professionalism, and certainly for church members. He was in for a rude awakening.

"When we got to the desk, [Houteff and the retired minister who referred him]," he wrote, "the sanitarium clerk asked me what kind of a deposit I could leave for admission. I said, 'a check.' It somewhat surprised me, for I had been in a hospital before but was never asked to pay anything in advance,—no, not even when I was dismissed. They sent me the bill by mail. When he saw that the check was drawn on an Illinois bank, I had to explain that I was somewhat new in the west and had not yet transferred my bank account. The clerk reluctantly took the check, and I was assigned to a room, and politely told that I had to wait for the doctor until he should come around.

"Well I waited all that day, but not a soul came in! In the evening, as sick as I was, I put on my clothes and went for supper into the dining room. Then I was told that the doctor was away, but he would see me just as soon as he came back. For four days this went on, and not a soul came into my room! I could have died and no one would have known it until perhaps days after. I suppose they had to get the money from the bank and find out if my credit was good before they would give me service!

"Finally on the fourth day, the sanitarium chaplain came with apologies for his delay to see me. 'If I had known that you were a Seventh-day Adventist,' he explained, 'I would have seen you sooner.' I was not expecting him, though, and it did not make much difference with me. But I said to myself, if you did not know what I was, you should have come sooner.

"At last the doctor came and after a thorough examination, I was told that I was a very sick man and had to have a special day and night nurse to look after me and to give me hydrotherapy treatments. With my consent a student nurse came in. But when the shadows of evening stretched over the sky, the nurse told me that they were short of special nurses, and so he himself was to wait on me all through the night if I let him move his cot into my room. All the time I was there, though, he never once got up at night to wait on me.

"Thus I had a private day and night nurse, and in the end I was charged .50 an hour—six dollars daily for him to wait on me during the day time, and six dollars nightly for sleeping with me in the room! This along with the additional charges was a heavy drain on my already dwindling savings. And the picture of growing broke and of staying poor grew larger and larger in my own mind, but I recovered from my illness, and was thankful.

"This sanitarium incident, though, produced another disappointing picture in my mind. Is that sanitarium God's place for His sick people? I asked myself. Is this people really God's people? The answer that came to these questions was this: The sanitarium is God's, and the church is God's, but the people that are running them are reactionaries, they are the modern priests, scribes and Pharisees, that there is a need for more Samaritans among them. This is where God's truth is, though, and God helping me, I said, I shall stay with it.

Yes, God did help me, I kept the faith, complained about nothing and stayed in the church with as good record as any.

"After I left the hospital, however, I was weak and my bank account was almost depleted. It appeared to me, too, that there was nothing that I could get into with the Sabbath [Saturday] off, that I would fall to the mercy of some charity, or else starve.

Moreover, for several months I had sent neither tithes [specified donations] nor my pledges of offerings to the church in the middle west, consequently, I owed something like $75. I thought then that if I should fail to pay this debt now while I had enough to pay it, I could never again get that much money together and it would have to stay unpaid forever. Better get broke now, I said, and be free of debt than to get broke later and to be a debtor forever.

"My bank account, I figured, was just a little over my debt. When I wrote a check for the whole balance and sent it to the church in the middle west, I was left with $3.50 in my pocket, and with no prospect of a job. Then I wrote to the bank in the middle west that I was closing my account, and that they should send the canceled checks and other papers to my address in California." (7)

He had reached the bottom. He was nearly penniless. His material hopes appeared dashed to pieces. His health was apparently gone, and like the Greek Orthodox Church, the Adventist Church had bitterly disappointed him. It is often when men reach their lowest ebb, their extremity, that they find a hope beyond understanding. When grief holds the heart with an iron grip; when nothing seems desirable in life; when one's dreams and dearest aspirations have shattered, then appears the working of more than normal power, arms that lift the soul above earthly trials. When men grasp this aid they really touch God. This is what Houteff believed he did - he touched God. It was then that he gripped, what he would term, omnipotence. It is when men have such an experience that they can become truly great - they can change the world. Whether in life or in death, their example affects thousands or millions doing what seems to be more than human effort.

Why did they treat him with such neglect? Was it simply

financial—his not having an account with a local bank? Did they need to secure funds from the Illinois bank, before starting treatment? Was it because he spoke with a foreign accent? Whatever the reason, nothing seems to justify their supineness. Nevertheless, evidence shows that this experience did not embitter Houteff toward the church or anyone. He was certainly disappointed and displeased, but bitter? No! He saw inconsistencies, faults, and failings; but this was not the primary reason for his eventual call for reformation within the church. Instead as his own testimony verified, he determined to stay with the church because he believed it was God's special instrument to represent His truth for the time. This Houteff held with all confidence until his death.

Looking back on the experience, Houteff said, "no, there is neither beast nor man that can take your life or cheat you of promotion if you do God's bidding, if you know that He Who keepeth Israel neither sleeps nor slumbers (Ps. 121:3, 4); that He knows all about you, my friends, every moment of the day and of the night; that He takes notice even of the hairs that fall from your heads; that whatever befalls you is but God's own will for your own good. I say, if you know and believe that He is God and the Keeper of your bodies and souls, then regardless what befalls you, you will be happy in it and give God the credit for it, not murmuring, but glorying even in your trails and afflictions." (11)

"At this point of my life, though, the table turned around as much as it turned with Abraham after he had done all but slay his son Isaac on the altar of God. Just a few days after I had written to the bank I heard from them, and to my great surprise they had enclosed a check for about $350 as my final balance! I never discovered how it happened."

"In the meantime, I got a job in a washing machine agency, and just then the Seventh-day Adventists were having their 1923 camp meeting in Los Angeles. And so I decided to attend and between meetings to try to sell Maytag washers in the neighborhood. And what do you suppose? I sold a washer a day and a few vacuum cleaners on the side. This went on all the while the camp lasted, and my first check from the company was about $425. But this was not all, just then another surprise overtook me. Some years before, I had bought stock which I had made up my mind was worthless, but to my surprise I received a letter in which the corporation inquired if I would like to sell it back to them, and the price they offered was more than double the price which I had paid!"

"Moreover, this Maytag agency was new, and when I went to work for them, they had but a small place. All the while I worked for them, though, they prospered and grew as did Laban while Jacob worked for him. In three years they opened branch offices all over the vicinity of Los Angeles, and then erected a building of their own which looked like a bank inside and out, one block deep and something like sixty feet wide." (12)

After having great success selling washing machines, he began experimenting with selling health sweets. In fact, he nearly stopped selling washing machines and launched full time into selling health candies—plus canvassing for the church—selling S.D.A. books and periodicals.

Houteff's faith strengthened in the Adventist message. His zeal and love for God and the church soared. He subjected his entire life to his beliefs. For example, he kept the Sabbath (Saturday). Seventh-day Adventists believe in the Biblical Sabbath, that secular activities should be set aside during Sabbath hours (sunset Friday—sunset Saturday). Activities are only engaged in which cannot be performed on other days; or which are of necessity; or which are religious in nature. Adventists believe, according to scripture, that the Sabbath is still binding upon all today, and God never changed it. It is part of the Ten Commandments God wrote with His own finger and gave to Moses.

Hence, no matter the cost, or risk, or personal sacrifice one must obey God's word. Not all Adventists are faithful to this and other standards, but Houteff certainly was. He, like all committed believers, believed God would always provide for their needs when they placed His work or His wishes above their own. They believe that God loves them, and though tests and trials may come, He had vowed to never forsake them—a lesson brought home to Houteff through several experiences. None more potent, perhaps, than those of this period of his life.

"My unexpected success in selling washing machines," he wrote, "of course, was used as a boost pump to the other salesmen, and the sales manager became very inquisitive about my religion. The last I talked with him he said to me: 'Houteff, it must be wonderful to believe as you do, but you know I could never be a Seventh-day Adventist.' I asked why could he not be, and he replied: 'Because if I begin to keep the Sabbath as you do I will lose my job.'

"I said, 'It is better to lose your job than to lose your life.' And the conversation ended. But the next time I went into the office I saw a wreath hanging on the door, and everything seemed to be upset. Then I was told that Mr. Harney, the sales manager, had suddenly taken sick the night before and died early that morning."

"About that time the head bookkeeper, too, became interested in discussing religion with me. As time went on, I discussed the same I had discussed with Mr. Harney, and at last he, too, said, 'Houteff, it must be wonderful to feel as you do, but I could never be a Seventh-day Adventist.'

"I said, 'Why?'

"Oh, I could not keep the Sabbath and my job, too,' he replied.

"'Well,' I said, 'it is better to lose your job than to lose your life, Mr. Barber.'

"And surely enough, the next time I went into the office I found everybody talking instead of working! Then I was told that Mr. Barber, the head bookkeeper, was found dead that morning in his room! Believe it or not, but this is what happened with both men after they sold their convictions for the price of a job!

Coupled with these events, Houteff continued telling how his life had completely turned around.

"A little later, I thought that I should have something of my own instead of continuing to work for Mr. Sleuter. So I was spending most of my time with experiments on health sweets, and as I then sold a washer only now and then, I was not too popular with the company. And as the company owed me some commissions, I decided to find out why were they held back. After discussing the matter several times with the sales manager he put me off each time with a promise to 'see to it.' But one day I pressed the matter harder, and as a result he said, 'Houteff, I am tired with this and I don't care, you can quit.' Next time I went in, I learned that Mr. Lisco, the sales manager, was discharged and that Mr. Foster had taken his post. Mr. Lisco, you see, was the one who had to quit, not I.

"I then went to see their new manager about my commissions. He promised to investigate the matter and to let me know the next time I came in. He, though, did the same thing Mr. Lisco did. And when I pressed the matter as hard as I did with Mr. Lisco, he, too, said, 'Houteff, I am tired with the thing, and do not care if you quit.' Peculiarly enough, though, the next time I went in, I was told that Mr. Foster, the sales manager, was discharged and was no longer with the company. I still was.

"By this time I had created enough business with my health sweets to keep busy and was about to quit altogether. I then went to see Mr. Sleuter himself about the aforementioned commissions, but he received me very coldly, and plainly told me that I had nothing coming. I quit. But in the space of less than about six months, I think it was, he lost the agency and another man took over the company. This is the way his prosperity ended." (13)

You may or may not agree with his assessment of the situation, but let no one think that Houteff was fanatical or imbalance in his religious experience or practice. His life's record made that point clear. Actually, he despised and untiringly rebuked every species of fanaticism—that plague of nearly every movement and scourge of every attempt at proper, beneficial reform.

On the other hand, he believed fervently that God was real, a personable, loving, all powerful Being, a Heavenly Father who covered every facet of His children's existence. This belief took on new meaning one Wednesday afternoon when he crossed a busy intersection in downtown Los Angeles. Describing the incident, he wrote the following.

"One Wednesday I drove to the business section of Los Angeles. Having finished my business quite late in the afternoon, and while walking across a street, I saw a woman driving toward me. But as I was almost to the middle of the street, I saw no danger for there was plenty of room for her to drive by. She nevertheless turned her car right square into me. Yes, she struck me from my left, and being overly excited she could not stop her car before she reached the middle of the block. And so she kept on going from the corner of the street to the middle of the alley. What happened to me when the car struck me? Did it lay me flat on the street, and did it run over me? No, this did not happen because something greater took place."

"An unseen hand carried me on ahead of the car, lightly sliding my feet on the pavement with my right side ahead, and my left side against the car's radiator! After having made about half the distance before the car stopped, something seated me on the bumper of the car, and I put my left arm around the car's left headlight. Then I said to myself, 'Now lady you can keep on going if that is the best you can do.' When she stopped, I put my feet on the ground and stepped away from the car.

"Just then I discovered that the pencil I had in my coat pocket had broken into half a dozen pieces from the impact, but my ribs were untouched! By that time the car and I were surrounded with people, and three policemen searching for the man that got run over. But as they found no one lying on the street, or pinned under the car, I told them that it was I who had been run over. They wanted to take me to the hospital, and when I told them that I was not hurt, I heard one say, 'He must be hurt but is too excited and does not know his condition.'" (14)

It was about this time, 1928 and 1929, when a series of denominational lesson studies were formulated from the Old Testament book of Isaiah. The lessons were based upon the expositions of a prominent SDA church leader, M.L. Andreason, and his book, "Isaiah The Gospel Prophet." This book became the source of the lesson's interpretation of Isaiah. The book and lessons were sanctioned and widely accepted by the Seventh-day Adventist church's General Conference and Sabbath school departments worldwide.

Although the lessons presented traditional, orthodox, Biblical Adventist theology, it presented new concepts, broader interpretations of the book of Isaiah. Isaiah's prophecies speak of a glorious ending for the saints. They reveal a church filled with the glory of heaven, and righteousness shining forth in a world of darkness and confusion. They spread hope and peace to all who desire the kingdom of the Messiah. Andreason emphasized that this would begin prior to the return of Christ. Traditional emphasis normally placed this beginning after the return of Christ.

These broader, clearer views of Isaiah's writings had deep effects upon many minds and Christian experiences. However, none so deep as Houteff's. As a Sabbath school teacher, he studied and prepared these lessons for his class, deeply impressed by the light flooding his mind as he contemplated these glorious themes. Although God's people would face "a time of trouble" and persecution, Houteff was convinced that the gospel dispensation would end in greater triumph than when it began. Not that the early church's experience was short of grandeur by any means. The biblical record shows marvelous miracles, wildfire growth, burning throughout the Roman Empire. A force that for centuries Rome tried to snuff out by killing thousands upon thousands of martyrs. But Rome failed to destroy Christianity.

Isaiah's prophecies seemed to portray a church that would not taste death. But in the midst of persecution, God's people filled with His goodness, faith, and love would go forth as a mighty, "bulletproof" army, proclaiming the gospel. As a result millions would quickly commit their lives to God and embrace the gospel. All of this was preadvent as opposed to the traditional theology of the church's persecution hiding in caves and hills where few (144,000) would remain alive. Houteff was convinced that the 144,000 were only the first portion of souls in the great harvest. Instead the final gospel harvest would include a great multitude—millions and millions from every "nation, tongue, and people." (Rev. 7:9)

Scripture animated his mind, and soul. Portraitures not only rooted in Isaiah, but also in the writings of nearly all the ancient seers. Finally there would be a people on this earth who would perfectly represent God, who would love as Jesus loved, who would be true and faithful. A people who cannot be bribed, adulated or intimidated into wrong. They would rather perish than violate their conscience— pure examples of true Christianity. At last, all honest, truth-seekers would recognize Christ's character shining in His people, embrace the gospel, accept God personally, swell the ranks of God's household, ushering in the second coming of Christ foretold in the New Testament. There was no doubt in Houteff's mind that this was God's plan.

In order for these events to occur, the sad state which then permeated the denomination had to cease.

The denomination needed a revival and reformation—a reorganization. There is no question that, in the late 20s and 30s, the Seventh-day Adventist denomination slid from many of its earlier standards. The church at large had adopted customs and practices that were leading it down a path of lost peculiarity, lost simplicity of faith.

Houteff was captivated. More and more his heart became ebullient. The lessons became fuller, richer, deeper. The Bible became a new book. Its pages flowered with new revelations—truth, he was convinced, needed by his church, needed by all Christendom. Houteff felt as though he was being guided and directed by a heavenly influence, a power beyond earthly intelligence, revealing scripture in a light never before seen. Issues of life and death were made plain.

He knew then that somehow he was privileged to be a chosen channel for a special "end-time" message. A message of hope, yet of stern rebuke. A message sublime and sweet, yet it would bring bitter opposition. A message demanding change and repentance, yet it would encapsule and crystallize the dreams and visions of the ancients.

Could he refuse to proclaim it? Could he sit in silence and ignore the heavenly call? He was not a pastor or conference official. He was not formally trained in theology, to preach or teach. He was a respected Sabbath-school teacher and an assistant Sabbath-school superintendent, yet, he was only a laymember. Why would they listen to him?

But, Houteff could not refuse the call. The message he felt was not his but God's, and he was constrained to declare it. Regardless of cost he would be true to his divine injunction. Many of the prophets were men of humble origin. What of the apostles? Poor, ignorant fishermen, except for a few, they, too, lacked formal education.

Declaring the manner of Paul's preaching, didn't the scriptures say, "Where is the wise? where is the scribe? where is the disputer of this world? hath not God made foolish the wisdom of this world?" (15)

Each Sabbath Houteff taught his Sabbath-school class the insights he had gained on Isaiah, chapters 54-66. As news spread of this new illumination, members came, hungry for what some Christians call the "meat of the Word," until Houteff's class grew considerably. Out of a 200 member church, about 60 joined his class. That's nearly triple standard membership for an adult class.

Soon it was suggested that Houteff hold an afternoon class in the church instead of a morning class. Next he was requested to move to a smaller classroom. It was said that the young people needed the auditorium in the afternoon. The smaller classrooms were too small for the burgeoning class. As the local leadership became increasingly disturbed about Houteff's phenomenal teaching success, they determined to halt his activities brick-wall his activities and draw attention back to themselves. On one pretext or another they stopped Houteff's class from meeting on church grounds.

However one class member, Mrs. C.E. Charboneau, owner of a large house across the street, welcomed the class. The Charboneaus became pioneers of the Davidian Movement and among the twelve that founded the original Mt. Carmel Center, where a street was named after them. As membership swelled, subtle opposition became more blatant. Church leaders denounced the special meetings and ostracized attendees. Fear of persecution stopped some. Curiosity brought others to fill their ranks. The overflow listened from outside through open windows. The church was in an uproar and divided—some for the meetings, some against.

About this time Houteff wrote, "Next they forbade us to attend their church services, and they began to disfellowship those who still wanted to attend our meetings. They tried to deport me, too, but failed. Then they endeavored to get a court order against any of us going to the church on Sabbath, but lost out. Once they called the police to have me arrested on false charges that I was disturbing the meetings, but after the officers in the police station heard my story and the deacon's charges against me, he commanded the two policemen who brought us to the station to put us in their car again, and to take us right back to the church where they picked me up.

"After this the elders endeavored to put me in an insane asylum. The "city manager" of Glendale, himself a Seventh-day Adventist, had come to this church that Sabbath morning to lay down the charges and to see me carried away and locked in the asylum. After talking with me for a few minutes, though, the officer did nothing but to tell me that he would not bother me again. Then the 200 lb. city manager felt smaller than my 135 lb. weight.

"They did all these unbecoming things and many others; besides, they talked and preached against me. And though I had no one but the Lord to defend me at any time, yet in all these the victory was mine!" (16, 17)

The message spread. Adventist churches throughout the Los Angeles area heard about the unique studies. To some minds it was clear that the Lord had sent a message to His people. To others, he was a devil. But to more than a few, Houteff was the avenue by which a flood of heavenly light had illumined their souls. Believers were not looking to follow or idolize a man. In fact, Houteff, himself, constantly steered people away from every species of flattery or praise. Something he did throughout his ministry.

If one wanted a fetish, there were many human wonders in the church to idolize—popular and brilliant orators, men of renown, men of superior intellect and talent. Why choose a man who apparently had none of the above? Houteff was neither tall, commanding or particularly charismatic. What then drew people to his meetings and to his message? Curiosity? Novelty? Excitement? Perhaps, for some, it may have been so at first. But what kept them listening, studying, returning for more when the gales of persecution blew and opposition swirled around adherents? The compulsion was the message. Testimonies of adherents say that the overwhelming evidence constrained you. If you believed the Bible, believed in the inspired comments of the church's primary founder, accepted the fundamental teachings of Seventh-day Adventists (SDAs), desired to know and to love plain truth, you were compelled to acknowledge divine inspiration in this message. You'd recognize its author, not a little man from the Rhodope Mountains of Bulgaria, but the Author of authors, the God of all. Even an atheist wouldn't take long to recognize that this was no ordinary man. Whether you agreed or disagreed, his message affected you, stirred you.

Determined to squelch what they viewed as the lunatic ravings of a disgruntled member, church authoritarians, without official investigation, pronounced the message erroneous, excommunicating any of its supporters.

In June, 1930, Houteff compiled the early phase of his message in manuscript form and titled it—"The Shepherd's Rod." He placed a total of 33 hectographed copies with various SDA leaders at the General Conference Committee held in San Francisco. He asked them to carefully investigate its contents. The recipients promised to do so and make their findings known to him by letter or in person.

The title "Shepherd's Rod" would later be used to identify believers as well as the message. To denominational leaders, its adherents were "offshoots," "a lunatic fringe." The message was heretical, a threat to unity. While they hoped the whole issue would go away, others risked estrangement and accepted the message with remarkable glee.

Houteff pointed out that the name, "Shepherd's Rod," evolved from what he cited as a providential coincidence. In the Old Testament, the book of Micah refers to a "rod" that speaks and is capable of being heard. (Micah 6:9, KJV) "The Lord's voice crieth unto the city, and the man of wisdom shall see thy name: hear ye the rod, and who hath appointed it."

Referring to this, he stated, "The Lord declares that His voice is crying to the city (to the church), and that the men of wisdom shall see the name, and shall hear the Rod and Him Who hath appointed it.

"Manifestly, this rod is capable of speaking and of being heard, thus the command 'Hear ye the rod.' So far as we know, the only rod that has ever spoken is 'The Shepherd's Rod.' Moreover, it was not the results of any studious searching of the Bible that the book was so named, the author was not familiar with this scripture, nor did he have any understanding of the book of Micah at the time the title 'Shepherd's Rod' was given to the book." (19)

The term "Shepherd's Rod," itself, carried the heart of the message. The ancient shepherd was a patient, tender, long-suffering caretaker of his sheep— creatures prone to stray, to get trapped in thickets, to get lost, or fall prey to wild beasts. The shepherd used his staff (rod) to guide strays back to the safe path, or to ward off attackers. The psalmist, David, used, what we've come to know as the 23rd Psalm, to express God as the Divine Shepherd: "Thy rod and Thy staff they comfort me." (20)

Hebrew shepherds had their sheep pass under the rod in counting the tithe—that portion which belonged to the Lord. The Old Testament shows that Moses used a miracle-working shepherd's rod to deliver ancient Israel from Egyptian bondage and part the Red Sea. (21) The rod, then, becomes a symbol of comfort, power, and deliverance.

Although all promised to reply, only two of the 33 conference officials who received copies of the manuscript responded. F.C. Gilbert was one. In his brief letter of June 26, 1930 to Houteff he confesses that he didn't make a thorough study of the manuscript. He avoided addressing main points, but focused his unfavorable assessment on minor points.

Negative statements Gilbert made regarding the new message were his personal opinion. (22) Yet, many ministers gave the impression that Gilbert spoke for the General Conference Committee. If Elder Gilbert saw no validity in the message, then many church members felt free to disregard it altogether.

Houteff questioned the wisdom in this. "Have the people of

the whole denomination succumbed to the brain of one man? Is Elder Gilbert to dictate from now on as to what shall and what shall not be brought before God's people? If so, then think in what fearful jeopardy is our eternal welfare!" (23)

The manuscript touched several Biblical topics. However, its central theme was the 144,000 of the apocalyptic book, Revelation (chapter seven) relative to today's church. Elder Gilbert did not tackle that subject at all.

Although most church officials ignored the new message, some studied it in-depth. Unlike F.C. Gilbert, E.T. Wilson, conference president for the Carolinas, investigated the message thoroughly. In some respects his response, in a Dec. 15, 1933 letter to Houteff, mirrored emotions of many who would later embrace the controversial teachings.

"I might say that when I first looked at the 'Shepherd's Rod,' the very name seemed to prejudice me, and I came near tearing it up several times before I really read it, but each time, when I was about to destroy the book, the thought would come to me that this is against my principle, and I would lay the book away again. When I finally did read it, I was startled, and many times I would cry out to God to forgive me for my sins as a minister, if He were really speaking to me through this little volume, and when I finished it, I was convinced that I was reading no ordinary book, but being very cautious about seeming error, I began the second reading, making comparison with the Bible and the Testimonies [considered to be inspired commentaries on the Bible to SDAs] to be sure they were in harmony, but before each reading, I would cry to God to 'reveal truth and unmask error,' according to His promise..." (25) Brackets added.

E.T. Wilson became a life-long devoted advocate of the "Shepherd's Rod" and the vice-president for the Davidian Association. It was E.T. Wilson who would later on perform Houteff's marriage in 1937.

W.F. Butterbaugh, MD, a reputed student of the Scriptures, and a former teacher in a SDA college, responded to Houteff in a general letter. Undated, addressed, "To Whom This May Concern," the letter is believed to have been written in the early 1930s. A following paragraph of which sufficiently shows his impressions.

"After a week of careful [group] study of three sessions daily, preceded by prayer, all present participating in beseeching the Lord that through His Holy Spirit He might direct in the discovery of truth, and that error, if such there be, might be made manifest, it was mutually agreed upon, that aside from typographical error, and in some cases of incorrect English, also certain historical statements of which we could neither affirm nor deny: and furthermore, it being ascertained that the author had never heretofore been associated with spiritualism in any of its forms, and as every study enlarged by exceeding great light upon the "Three Angels' Messages," also many vital and controverted points that have been perplexing mysteries were perfectly cleared up, there was left no question of doubt in our minds that these volumes have been prepared under some form of divine enlightenment; and that the time is fully ripe for the unfolding of these truths to a perishing world." (25) Brackets added.

Thousands of similar letters would be written in subsequent years, and literature distributed in the millions throughout the denomination. A movement was born that would shake Adventism from "center to circumference," that caused "scholarly Americans to scratch their heads." Though small in number, its members were strong in dedication, facing fierce opposition from clergy and laity. Though hounded by hatred, ostracized, and misrepresented, it continued to rise, and to prick the conscience of thousands worldwide.

Today, it survives in steadily growing numbers in North and South America, Africa, Europe, South Pacific, and the Far East but not without first withstanding lions of balking disillusionment.

On February 5, 1955, Victor T. Houteff died at the Hilcrest Hospital, Waco, Texas. He believed what many adherents believed then and now—in spite of set-backs, disappointments, opposition—one day the church and the secular world will witness fulfillment of prophecies recorded in Scripture. Prophecies elucidated by a series of messages termed the "Shepherd's Rod" written by a little man from Bulgaria. They will come to find that instead of a "madman," idealist or misguided zealot, he was a prophet without honor.

Chapter 3

A Unique Heritage

Today Seventh-day Adventists (SDAs) number 7,000,000—9,000,000 world-wide. They operate numerous medical facilities, colleges, academies, and thousands upon thousands of churches. They are an accepted fabric in the modern-day quilt of Christianity. But it was not always so.

To fully understand and appreciate the present, one must walk streets of the past. To truly understand Davidian Seventh-day Adventists (DSDAs) and their struggles, one must view briefly the history of Adventism itself.

William Miller, a Baptist preacher, born in Pittsfield, Massachusetts, became the father of modern Adventism. Although there were two Baptist ministers in the family, a grandfather and uncle, William's father cold-shouldered religion. However his devout mother nurtured William with Christianity's milk. (1)

William Miller's intellectual and spiritual strengths surfaced early. Between the ages of 7 and 10, he faced his first spiritual struggle. Recalling the time he says: "I spent much time in trying to invent some plan, whereby I might please God.... Two ways suggested themselves to me, which I tried. One was to be very good, to do nothing wrong, tell no lies, and obey my parents. But I found my resolutions were weak, and soon broken. The other was sacrifice; by giving up the most cherished objects I possessed. But this also failed me." (1)

After Miller married and moved to Poultney, Vermont, his spiritual confusion escalated. He read the writings of Voltaire, David Hume, Thomas Paine, Ethan Allen and became an avowed deist. Deism presented a then fashionable, rationalistic view of God. William often amused his deist friends by mimicking the piety of his religious relatives. (1)

The War of 1812 engulfed the country. As a commissioned Army captain, Miller fought in the battle of Plattsburgh in upstate New York. British forces outnumbered the Americans nearly three to one.

A cannonball fired from a British ship on Lake Champlain thudded two feet from him. Unhurt by exploding fragments raining around him, Miller wondered, Why? Could it be that the God he rejected, whose people he ridiculed, really cared about him and the country he loved? (49)

In 1815, discharged from the army, Miller and family moved to Low Hampton, New York. He built a house and settled into respectable citizenhood. Farming 200 acres, he established himself in the community. Reflecting on his life and wartime experiences, Miller returned slowly to his childhood faith with greater understanding and devotion.

Discovering that his deist views provided no assurance of happiness beyond the present life, he embraced intense Bible study. Astonished he said, "I saw that the Bible did bring to view just such a Savior as I needed; and I was perplexed to find how an uninspired book should develop principles so perfectly adapted to the wants of a fallen world." (1)

Miller reasoned that if the Bible were true it must be consistent and harmonious with itself. "Give me time," he declared, "and I will harmonize all those apparent contradictions to my own satisfaction, or I will be a deist still." Miller set aside all preconceived opinions and resolved to study the Bible for what it claimed to be—the Word of God. (1)

After years of painstaking study, Miller concluded that the Bible fulfilled Its claims. Scripture was Its own expositor—even when apparently clothed in mystical or cryptic language. He discovered that, except where figures or symbols were employed, the Bible should be taken exactly as It reads. (2)

Bible prophecies riveted Miller's attention, particularly a time prophecy in the eighth chapter of Daniel, which he realized had not met fulfillment. It read: "Unto two thousand and three hundred days; then shall the sanctuary be cleansed." (3)

Miller was convinced that this prophecy referred to the visible second advent of Christ. He believed that Jesus would return and take His people to the portals above for 1,000 years (or a millennium). During which, the earth would be desolate. After which, God would restore the earth to its pristine beauty, making it the eternal home of His people.

Conclusions contrary to popular views of the spiritual reign of Christ—a temporal millennium before the world comes to its end.

Miller stated, "I found that Jesus will again descend to this earth, coming in the clouds of heaven, in all the glory of His Father." He was firmly convicted that this "second advent" would happen soon (1843 or 1844). His preaching these convictions ignited a religious awakening like a match to dry grass, leaving an indelible mark on Christianity.

"I need not speak of the joy that filled my heart in view of the delightful prospect, nor of the ardent longing of my soul for a participation in the joys of the redeemed. The Bible was now to me a new book. It was indeed a feast of reason; all that was dark, mystical or obscure, to me, in its teachings, had been dissipated from my mind before the clear light that now dawned from its sacred pages; and oh, how bright and glorious the truth appeared! All the contradictions and inconsistencies I had before found in the word were gone; and, although there were many portions of which I was not satisfied I had a full understanding, yet so much light had emanated from it to the illumination of my before darkened mind, that I felt a delight in studying the Scriptures which I had not before supposed could be derived from its teachings. I commenced their study with no expectation of finding the time of the Savior's coming, and I could at first hardly believe the result to which I had arrived; but the evidence struck me with such force that I could not resist my convictions. I became nearly settled in my conclusions, and began to wait, and watch, and pray, for my Savior's coming." (4)

Following his rule of making Scripture its own interpreter, Miller learned that a day in symbolic prophecy represents a year. He saw that the period of 2300 prophetic days, or literal years, would extend far beyond the close of the Jewish dispensation, hence it could not refer to the sanctuary of that dispensation. Miller accepted the generally received view, that in the Christian age the earth is the sanctuary, and he therefore understood that the cleansing of the sanctuary foretold in Dan. 8:14 represented the purification of the earth by fire at the second coming of Christ. If, then, the correct starting-point could be found for the 2300 days, he concluded that the time of the second advent could be readily ascertained. (5) It was 1818, Miller's heart beat with rhythmic joy over what he concluded was prophetic revelations. His faith in and love of the Bible and Its promises seasoned every conversation. At first Miller promulgated his findings privately, hoping some minister would make them public. But he couldn't shake the calling.

In 1831, a 50-year-old Miller, presented his views publicly. His first lecture garnered invitations to preach in other areas. His preaching swept the continent with revival, converting hundreds in town after town.

"Liquor-dealers abandoned the traffic, and turned their shops into meeting-rooms; gambling dens were broken up; infidels, deists, Universalists, and even the most abandoned profligates were reformed, some of whom had not entered a house of worship for years. Prayer-meetings were established by the various denominations, in different quarters, at almost every hour, business men assembling at midday for prayer and praise." Miller received his ministerial license from the Baptist church in 1833. (6)

1840 marked rapid increase of Miller's work with far reaching results. Thousands upon thousands, worldwide, expected the Lord's soon return. In distant lands, wherever missionaries penetrated so went the message.

Miller's wasn't the only proclamation. Between 1821 and 1845, Dr. Joseph Wolff sounded a similar alarm. Wolff—German-born son of a Jewish rabbi—had embraced Protestantism early in life and united with the English church. After two years' study, in 1821, he traveled as missionary to Africa, Egypt, Abyssinia, Asia, Palestine, Syria, Persia, Bokhara, India and the United States.

The litany of proclaimers included Lacunza, a Spanish Jesuit; Bengal of Germany; Gaussen of France, whose writings also reached Scandinavia. Tidings had spread throughout the civilized world, attracting all classes to the Adventist meetings. (7)

Like Miller these proponents were dynamos defending and propelling the movement. Their Scripture knowledge was unsurpassed, their lives exemplary. One author, Ellen White, a prominent leader in early Adventism who took part in the movement related her feelings, "Of all the great religious movements since the days of the apostles, none have been more free from human imperfection and the wiles of Satan than was that of the autumn of 1844. Even now, after the lapse of many years, all who shared in that movement and who have stood firm upon the platform of truth, still feel the holy influence of that blessed work, and bear witness that it was of God." (8)

In an estimated 4,500 sermons between 1832 and 1844 to approximately half a million people, Miller pictured the glorious return. He withstood storms of scoffing persecutors and numerous attempts on his life. His work climaxed in the "great disappointment" of October 22, 1844.

The 2300 days prophecy of Daniel reckoned in prophetic time to be 2300 years. Miller and his associates believed it began with the decree by the Medo-Persian Empire, allowing the Jewish exiles to rebuild Jerusalem, and extended into the last days of earth's history. (9, 10, 11)

The decree to rebuild Jerusalem was declared in 457 BC. Miller and others traced prophetic signposts, verifying their precision. Calculating 2300 years from 457 BC, they determined that the prophecy would terminate between the spring of 1843 and the fall of 1844.

But what was to take place at the end of this period? Did the sanctuary symbolize the earth as prevailing wisdom dictated? If so, this meant Christ's second coming and earth's cleansing. This assumption bore bitter disappointment, first tasted, March 21, 1844. Christ didn't come as expected. Amidst jeers and scoffing of a skeptical, reviling world, believers remained unmoved. After restudying their position, forward they marched with renewed energy and zeal, armed with a new phase of their message subsequently termed the "midnight cry."

Their litmus test came October 22, 1844. Somewhere within

that 24 hours, they expected the sky to blaze with glory, the earth to quake from sea to sea, and Christ to come. Hadn't they proclaimed the final warning to a dying world, converting thousands? Wouldn't they now see their Lord's return? No celestial fireworks; no terrestrial grumbling; no return to paradise; the sun set as on any other day—a bitter disappointment.

Hemorrhaging hope, believers staggered under the weight of this "great disappointment." "Now to turn again to the cares, perplexities and dangers of life, in full view of the jeers and revilings of unbelievers who now scoffed as never before, was a terrible trial of faith and patience." (12)

Immediately many fell away from the advent movement. Some became trapped in fanaticism. Others believed Jesus would still return very soon. But time took its prey through ostracism and ridicule. The movement appeared broken into various chips and chunks, carried away by winds of circumstance, relegated to history's back pages, cataloged under "the unfortunate" and forgotten.

Was the advent movement of the 1840s just another trophy for the secular shelf, displayed as testimony against Christianity's claim to divine guidance? Were Adventists duped by clever, coincidental interpretations of the Bible?

In spite of human error in prophetic interpretation, there were those whose faith was not shaken. Today, dedicated SDA's would tell you that outstanding, biblical personages often misunderstood God's plan. Knowledge is attained by progression; truth is progressive, some would argue. Reality is perceived and understood gradually. Science is not stagnant; neither is true religion, they would proclaim.

Ellen White, put it succinctly. "Men are instruments in the hand of God, employed by Him to accomplish His purposes of grace and mercy. Each has his part to act; to each is granted a measure of light, adapted to the necessities of his time, and sufficient to enable him to perform the work which God has given him to do." (13)

Victor Houteff made this point. "Still further, there are circumstances in connection with certain aspects of every message which necessitate clarification. Such clarification, however, can be no greater than the light which shines at the time. And the light may come solely from within the message itself or, again, it may derive from a limited understanding common to the time 'then present'—an understanding which the messenger himself shares." (14)

"[The Millerite Movement] caused a weaning of affections from the things of this world," wrote White, "a healing of controversies and animosities, a confession of wrongs, a breaking down before God, and penitent, brokenhearted supplications to Him for pardon and acceptance. It caused self-abasement and prostration of soul, such as we never before witnessed...." (8)

Thus the 1840's Adventist Movement was another wrung in the ladder. Its "great disappointment" spelled not the end but a new beginning. Some Adventists concluded that they had understood the prophecy aright regarding time but had misunderstood the predicted event. Drawing on tradition or preconception, somehow, they had missed the meaning of the "sanctuary." What followed stands today and continues to grow after 150 years—the Seventh-day Adventist Church.

Hiram Edson, an Adventist leader in Port Gibson, New York, had opened his home to believers on October 22, 1844 to await Christ's return. Midnight passed; dawn greeted an unchanged world. Baffled believers entered a barn and prayed for hours.

Later, Edson and a friend crossed an unharvested cornfield. Perhaps the ears of corn seemed to have rustled in reproachful protest, mocking their mistake. Perhaps the farm's pungent, earthy odors reminded them of where—by all reckoning—they should not be.

Then it happened. Heaven seemed to open as in a vision. In the middle of that cornfield, Hiram Edson and friend saw Christ entering the "most holy place" in the heavenly sanctuary. That was the event. Not the earth being cleansed but the heavenly sanctuary—of which Moses had made a copy in the wilderness. (15)

After careful study and research, Edson and others added new dimensions to their thinking. They concluded that Christ had begun His atoning ministry as our Heavenly-high Priest. Yes, Christ would come but not until He had completed this final phase of advocacy for mankind.

O.R.L. Crotier, a schoolteacher and dedicated believer, printed an Adventist journal known as the Day Star. Published in Cincinnati, Ohio, February 7, 1846, it sought to clarify the question of the sanctuary. (15) This boosted the Adventists' spirits—whose numbers had dwindled from thousands worldwide to a flagging fifty stateside. Estimated in 1846 this anemic number comprised small groups throughout the northeast.

Other inspiring encouragers sprang up. Their unique testimonies often bordered the supernatural. In fact, even before the disappointment, near the peak of the Advent Movement this phenomenon had begun.

In 1818 William Ellis Foy, the giver of one such testimony, was born to Joseph and Elizabeth Foy (free blacks) of Kennebee County near Augusta, Maine. William, the eldest of three Foy boys, married and moved to Boston, Massachusetts. He was a member of and later became a minister in the Freewill Baptist Church. (16)

In 1840 the Millerites held their first General Conference of Adventist at Chardon Street Chapel in Boston, not far from where Foy lived. (17) Hearing their message left its mark on Foy. He wrote, "I am now awaiting my coming Lord. Although before the Lord was pleased to show me these heavenly things, I was opposed to the doctrine of Jesus' near approach. I am now looking for that event." (18)

Prior to the great disappointment of 1844, Foy received at least three visions which convinced him of Christ's imminent return. The first took place January 18, 1842 on Southark Street, Boston while he was praying with a group of believers. (19) The second occurred February 4, 1842. The third came prior to October 22, 1844.

A local physician, Foy's wife, and other believers (a racially mixed group) witnessed the first vision. It lasted two and a half hours. Foy stood still, unmovable, seemingly far away. The physician present verified Foy's condition. (Though a mysterious phenomenon, the cessation of one or more vital signs during vision authenticates the experience.)

As Foy later related what he saw, the visions appeared to have followed a logical progression. The first revealed the Advent Movement severely tried, shaken, tested, but victorious at last. He saw God's people rejoicing in a newly restored earth—a reward of the faithful. The second and third visions spoke of the judgment.

Foy saw the righteous pass scrutiny of the Judge of the Universe. However, the unrighteous faced execution of God's judgment. Throughout the visions, God's love, mercy, and long suffering watch care over His children was prominent. But soon He must render justice. He was warning his people to prepare for difficult times ahead.

Foy all but buckled under the burden to relate his visions. He was a black man in a world of prejudice flagrant Sure, the Millerites fully embraced all races, including blacks, but would they believe God was using him? Especially when he must declare an unpopular message.

"But I was disobedient," Foy wrote, "setting upon this point for an excuse. That my guide did not command me so to do; and I thereby brought darkness and doubt upon my soul. But I could find no peace or comfort." (20)

Invitations to speak poured in, and Foy submitted. He related faithfully his visions, exhorting listeners to prepare for solemn events. Persecuted and ostracized throughout his travels, yet believing God was with him, he was comforted. His preaching and writings sustained many after the great disappointment.

Shortly before October 1844 Hazen Foss had also received a vision. It was strikingly similar to Foy's third which portrayed the Advent peoples' travels toward the City of God. Foss was a white, well-educated, accomplished speaker from a prominent Adventist family. Apparently ideal for a mouthpiece. Unlike Foy, Foss refused the job. He would not risk his reputation.

When given the vision a second time, itt was revealed to Foss that if he refused again, he would be released from the responsibility. It would be given to one of the "weakest of the Lord's children." (21)

When he refused again, he was told that "He was released,

and the burden was laid upon one of the weakest of the weak, who would do the Lord's bidding." (19) Those words chilled his bones, pride vanished. Foss decided there were worse things than ridicule. He called a public meeting determined to share the vision. Foss stood before the assembly dumb-founded. "I cannot remember a word of the vision." His anguished cry rang out. "God has fulfilled His word. He has taken the vision from me...I am a lost man." (21)

Foss lived another 50 years with no inclination for religion or spiritual things. He never attended another Adventist meeting and was reportedly in despair for the remainder of his life. Three months after refusing the call Foss met the "weakest of the weak," chosen to fill his place, Ellen Gould Harmon.

On November 26, 1827, Robert and Eunice Harmon graced Gorham, Maine with the birth of their twin daughters—Ellen and Elizabeth. The Harmons were vibrant members of the Methodist Episcopal Church in Gorham. While the twins were small, Robert Harmon moved his family of ten (8 children, 2 adults) to Portland, Maine. There they continued as members in the Methodist Episcopal. Then came 1843 and the Millerite Advent Movement. Accepting these radical ideas, caused the Harmons' excommunication from the Methodists—an unpleasant farewell.

One spring day in 1836, nine-year-old twins, Ellen and Elizabeth crossed a Portland common with a friend. A thirteen-year-old classmate accosted them angry over some trifle. The cardinal household rule: Never contend with anyone. If you're in danger in anyway, get home fast, rang in the twin's ears. "Run!"

Three pairs of feet pounded pavement, a fourth pair close behind. Ellen looked back to see how close—wrong move. Suddenly the female bully threw a stone and smashed Ellen's nose. Ellen never saw the road rise up to meet her. Gushing blood, she regained consciousness in a nearby shop. The owner tried to help as blood soaked her dress and puddled on his floor. A kind stranger offered a ride home in his carriage. Dazed, Ellen looked at all the blood. She couldn't soil his carriage. "I prefer to walk."

Unaware of the seriousness of her injury, they let her walk.

After a short distance, Ellen's vision blurred. She weaved, staggered, stumbled. Elizabeth and her school-friend carried Ellen home.

For three weeks she lay in a stupor almost "reduced to a skeleton." (22) Physician, friends, and family thought she wouldn't live. But Eunice Harmon felt her daughter would make it. Ellen's features were so altered by her broken nose, her father returned from a business trip and didn't know her.

Referring to this time years later, Ellen wrote: "My health seemed to be hopelessly impaired. For two years I could not breathe through my nose, and was able to attend school but little. It seemed impossible for me to study and to retain what I learned. The same girl who was the cause of my misfortune was appointed monitor by our teacher, and it was among her duties to assist me in my writing and other lessons. She always seemed sincerely sorry for the great injury she had done me, although I was careful not to remind her of it. She was tender and patient with me, and seemed sad and thoughtful as she saw me laboring under serious disadvantage to get an education.

"My nervous system was prostrated, and my hand trembled so that I made but little progress in writing, and could get no further than the simple copies in coarse hand. As I endeavored to bend my mind to my studies, the letters on the page would run together, great drops of perspiration would stand upon my brow, and a faintness and dizziness would seize me. I had a bad cough, and my whole system seemed debilitated. My teachers advised me to leave school and not pursue my studies further till my health should improve. It was the hardest struggle of my young life to yield to my feebleness and decide that I must leave my studies and give up the hope of gaining an education.

"Three years later I made another trial to obtain an education. But when I attempted to resume my studies, my health rapidly failed, and it became apparent that if I remained in school, it would be at the expense of my life. I did not attend school after I was twelve years old." (22)

By October 1844, a 17-year-old Ellen, excommunicated with her parents and siblings from the Methodist Church, awaited the Lord's return. In December, two months after the Great Disappointment, Ellen had the vision Hazen Foss refused to proclaim. On one occasion, when Ellen related what she had seen, Hazen Foss reportedly said: "That is the instrument on whom the Lord has laid the burden." He said that the vision was as near to that shown him as two persons could relate the same thing. It was what he could not remember after refusing the third call. (21)

Foss spoke to Ellen the next morning. "The Lord gave me a message to bear to His people, and I refused after being told the consequences. I was proud; I was unreconciled to the Disappointment. I murmured against God, and wished myself dead. Then I felt a strange feeling come over me. I shall be henceforth as one dead to spiritual things. I heard you talk last night. I believe the visions are taken from me, and given to you. Do not refuse to obey God, for it will be at the peril of your soul. I am a lost man. You are chosen of God; be faithful in doing your work, and the crown I might have had, you will receive."

Ellen's first vision described the Advent people traveling a narrow path toward heaven. Jesus was before them guiding their travels. The light set up behind them, at the beginning of the path, was identified as the message proclaimed just prior to the Great Disappointment—the midnight cry. She saw many grow weary and doubt the light behind them (Miller's message). The light which gave light to their feet went out leaving doubters in total darkness. They lost sight of Jesus, stumbled and fell off the path down into what she described as the "dark and wicked world below." (23)

The steadfast and faithful beheld their Lord coming in the clouds of glory to receive His weary but loyal people. They'd experience the glories of heaven for a thousand years then a new earth of perfect peace, ceaseless joy, and bliss. She mentioned the precise number of the redeemed, those who did not fall off the path—"the living saints, 144,000 in number." (23) The same number found in the last book of the Bible, Revelation 7:4.

While this vision did not provide reasons for the Disappointment, as Foy's had, it did provide assurance of God's leading and future victory. But the question remained: What should they do now? What was God's immediate plan? To some Hiram Edson's plausible explanation of the "heavenly sanctuary being cleansed" seemed acceptable. Befuddled, the believers prayed and studied Scripture for more direction.

A week after the first vision, Ellen received another. She saw views of the heartache, anguish, and opposition she'd experience. "But said the angel, 'The grace of God is sufficient for you; He will hold you up.' She wrote:

"After I came out of this vision, I was exceedingly troubled. My health was very poor, and I was but seventeen years old. I knew that many had fallen through exaltation, and I knew that if I in any way became exalted, God would leave me, and I should surely be lost. I went to the Lord in prayer and begged Him to lay the burden on someone else. It seemed to me that I could not bear it. I lay upon my face a long time, and all the light I could get was, 'Make known to others what I have revealed to you.' (24)

"The larger group who turned from confidence in the fulfillment of prophecy in 1844 numbered approximately thirty thousand. Their leaders came together in 1845 in a conference in Albany, New York, April 29 to May 1, at which time they restudied their positions. By formal action they went on record as warning against those who claim "special illumination," those who teach "Jewish fables," and those who establish "new tests" (Advent Herald, May 14, 1845).

They were confident that prophecy had not been fulfilled in 1844, and some set time for the termination of the 2300-day period in the future. Various times were set, but one after another they passed. These people, held together by the cohesive element of the Advent hope, at first aligned themselves in several rather loosely knit groups with considerable variation in certain doctrinal positions. Some of these groups soon faded out. (25)

Subsequently, in 1846 those who accepted the sanctuary teaching, the Sabbath, and Ellen White's prophetic gift numbered about 50. They often gathered in small groups in homes in the New England area for prayer and Bible study. They became the pioneers of the

Seventh-day Adventist Denomination. (26)

Most Seventh-day Adventist beliefs are common within Christendom. They believe "The Holy Scriptures of the Old and New Testaments were given by inspiration of God, and contain an all-sufficient revelation of His will to men, and is the only unerring rule of faith and practice." (27)

They believe in the Trinity, God is revealed as one in three: Father, Son (Jesus), and the Holy Spirit. That Jesus Christ is very God, not a created being, but of the same nature as the Father. He took on the nature of the human family; lived as a man; died for the salvation of mankind; rose again the third day; ascended into heaven; and will soon return. That every person, in order to receive salvation, must experience the New Birth. All must experience the entire transformation of life and character through the recreative power of God and faith in Jesus Christ.

They believe in baptism by immersion. And that a Christian is obligated to moral conduct as mandated in Scripture and summarized in the Decalogue (Ten Commandments) recorded by Moses. (27)

Understanding SDAs' five most distinctive doctrines is crucial to understanding the church that later confronted Victor Houteff. They are: (1) the Sabbath, (2) the sanctuary, (3) mortality of the soul, (4) advanced lifestyle reform, (5) the gift of prophecy in modern times.

To trace the inception of Sabbath observance, we go to a small church in New Hampshire approximately 60 miles from the New York state line. Here an independent Christian church accepted the Advent message in 1843. We find Rachel Preston Oakes, a Seventh-day Baptist in their midst, distributing tracts urging all to accept and keep the Biblical Sabbath (Saturday). The tracts showed that the Sabbath, as given in the Old Testament, was still binding. Several, both ministers and laity, were impressed and began keeping the Sabbath.

Frederick Wheeler was the first Adventist minister to accept the Biblical Sabbath. Another was T.M. Preble who discussed it in an article published in 1845. Joseph Bates read Preble's article and accepted the Sabbath. Bates published a 48-page pamphlet on the subject in August 1846. (28) Reading that pamphlet, convinced James and Ellen White of the Sabbath's importance. Ellen had previously met Bates, but wasn't impressed to keep Sabbath until after studying the Biblical evidence. (29)

James and Ellen had married August 30, 1846. The newly weds kept their first Sabbath in the autumn of that year. (30) Seven months later, Mrs. White was given a vision on its importance. This reinforced Advent believers convictions on the subject. The vision came after they studied Biblical evidence, and followed its teaching. In 1846 Mr. Crozier published findings on the Sabbath. He also published Mrs. White's visions, confirming their Biblical discoveries. (31)

The sanctuary question. Christ's moving into the Most Holy apartment of the heavenly temple to begin an "investigative judgment" became very popular among Adventists. They found substantial, Biblical support of this concept, making it the most distinctive mark of Seventh-day Adventists.

Ellen White summarized an explanation of the Great Disappointment and its relationship to the sanctuary dogma. "But clearer light came with the investigation of the sanctuary question. They now saw that they were correct in believing that the end of the 2300 days in 1844 marked an important crisis. But while it was true that that door of hope and mercy by which men had for eighteen hundred years found access to God, was closed, another door was opened, and forgiveness of sins was offered to men through the intercession of Christ in the most holy.... (32)

"The passing of the time in 1844 was followed by a period of great trial to those who still held the
advent faith. Their only relief, so far as ascertaining their true position was concerned, was the light which directed their minds to the sanctuary above." (33)

The pioneers marched forward proclaiming Christ's soon return. But they emphasized the needed preparation before He would close His mediatorial work and leave the "Most Holy Place."

Seventh-day Adventists do not believe death sends you immediately to heaven or hell as taught commonly by much of Christendom. They believe, from their study of biblical evidence, when you die your body turns to dust; your breath returns to Him who gave it—God. There is no consciousness after death—none. You sleep in the grave until the resurrection.

Seventh-day Adventists (SDAs) believe that the body is the temple of God for the indwelling of the Holy Spirit. (34) Thus, members are encouraged to practice advanced health and dress standards. Early believers ate as most of society did.

Beginning in 1863, continuing throughout her ministry, Mrs. White was shown in vision dietary reform. If followed, it would reverse the tidal wave decline of man's physical and spiritual health. At first clean foods, defined in the Old Testament, were accepted as a heavenly diet. Later, SDAs were urged to adopt a well-balanced, no flesh food, vegetarian regimen. Further dietary modifications excluded alcohol, tobacco, all caffinated beverages. Although not all adhere to the standards, SDAs are known in nutritional circles to live an average 7-9 years longer than the general population with fewer incidences of catastrophic diseases. Today's scientific findings appear to have validated Mrs. White's instructions with uncanny accuracy.

By 1867 dress reform was introduced promoting morality in modest apparel.

The fifth distinctive SDA belief is that the gift of prophecy did not die with the Bible prophets. Paul's writings assert that God ordained this gift remain with the church until Christ's return. God can and has chosen a person(s); given them ability to prophesy or predict events; discern things that the average person cannot.

Since the Bible is the final and supreme authority for the faithful, any prophet or prophecy must be in total harmony with it. His interpretation must be in concord with the whole tenor of Scripture; lead men in loyalty to the law and previous prophets; bring a message needful for the time and/or circumstances. Such a messenger does not supersede the Bible but acts as a magnifying glass, enlarging Bible themes. He neither adds to nor subtracts from Holy Writ.

Prophetic symbolism is a divine code dictated by God. Therefore, the Bible explains itself. Through the gift of prophecy God reveals the meaning of such symbols prior to the prophecy's fulfillment. For He does nothing before revealing it to His prophets who inform is people. (35) Thus a true or false prophet can be detected.

SDAs believe Mrs. White's 70 year ministry fits the true prophet's mold. Her writings if stacked one on top of the other would rise 7 ft. She made countless predictions, most already fulfilled, others bear future application. Her work has been acknowledged by scholars and circulated by the millions. Her primary means of divine communication was through visions. One of which George I. Butler witnessed in 1874 and gave this fascinating account.

"For nearly thirty years past these visions have been given with greater or less frequency, and have been witnessed by many, oftentimes by unbelievers as well as those believing them. They generally, but not always, occur in the midst of earnest seasons of religious interest while the Spirit of God is specially present.

"The time Mrs. White is in this condition has varied from fifteen minutes to one hundred and eighty. During this time the heart and pulse continue to beat, the eyes are always wide open, and seem to be gazing at some far-distant object, and are never fixed on any person or thing in the room. They are always directed upward. They exhibit a pleasant expression. There is no ghastly look or any resemblance of fainting. The brightest light may be suddenly brought near her eyes, or feints made as if to thrust something into the eye, and there is never the slightest wink or change in expression on that account....

"While she is in vision, her breathing entirely ceases. No breath ever escapes her nostrils or lips when in this condition. This has been proved by many witnesses, among them physicians of skill and themselves unbelievers in the visions, on some occasions being appointed by a public congregation for the purpose. Persons may pinch her flesh, and do things which would cause great and sudden pain in her ordinary condition, and she will not notice it by the slightest tremor....

"Peculiar circumstances in the lives of individuals, whom she never before had seen in the flesh, and secrets hidden from the nearest acquaintances have been made known by her when she had no personal knowledge of the parties other than by vision. Often has she been in an audience where she was wholly unacquainted with the individuals composing it, when she would get up and point out person after person whom she never had seen before, in the flesh, and tell them what they had done, and reprove their sins. I might mention many other items of like nature, but space forbids. These things can be proved by any amount of testimony, and we confidently affirm that they are of such a character that they could not be accomplished by deception." (36)

On several occasions, while in vision, Mrs. White held a large Bible in one hand at arms length. With the other hand she turned pages and pointed out various verses. Her eyes focused upward away from the Bible as she read.

The Harmon family Bible weighed 18 1/2 lbs. One morning in early 1845, while she was still living at home in Portland, Maine, Ellen was taken in vision. She stepped over to a bureau, lifted that heavy Bible, placed it in her left hand, and extended it arms length. Ellen held that closed book with ease for half an hour. During the vision, in short exclamations, she referred to the value of God's Word.

"Under ordinary circumstances she was unable to pick up this book, for she was in frail health and at that time weighed only eighty pounds. She was in no way fatigued by this experience." (37)

J.N. Loughborough gave an amusing account of one incident. "Before he had half completed his examination, he (Dr. Brown) turned deathly pale, and shook like an aspen leaf. Elder White said, 'Will the doctor report her condition?' He replied, 'She does not breathe,' and rapidly made his way to the door. Those at the door who knew of his boasting, said, 'Go back, and do as you said you would; bring that woman out of the vision.' In great agitation he grasped the knob of the door, but was not permitted to open it until inquiry was made by those near the door, 'Doctor, what is it?' He replied, 'God only knows; let me out of this house!'" (37)

Ellen White made astounding predictions concerning science, health, nutrition, medicine, narcotics, physiology, hypnosis, botany, and geology. Twentieth Century research validated her uncanny insights. Clive McCay, Ph.D., professor of nutrition at Cornell University, Ithaca, New York has recognized the wisdom of her instructions.

She wrote of fat, particularly animal fats, being associated with coronary heart disease and cardio-vascular disorders. She wrote of prenatal influences on the fetus. She wrote of the beneficial effect of sunlight. She wrote of the baleful effects of tobacco as a causative agent for cancer and respiratory diseases. She wrote of the dangerous effects of certain drugs, alcohol, and meats. They all came under her pen. Her counsel given in the mid-nineteenth century drew constant ridicule but does not today.

Her educational background was very limited. Yet, she baffled society with unprecedented foresight into fields she never formally studied—science, education, psychology...claiming God as her source of knowledge. She predicted future events—and did predict the San Francisco earthquake of April 18, 1906.

Ellen G. White had perhaps the most outstanding influence on Adventist theology and organization. She lived a life of simplicity, austerity, self-sacrifice, and devotion. She always gave respect to a higher power for all of her accomplishments. On July 16, 1915, at 3:40 p.m. this 87-year-old wonder uttered her last words. "I know in whom I believed. God is love. He giveth His beloved sleep." (38)

The Seventh-day Adventist denomination was formally organized in 1863. Since inception it has established educational and medical facilities worldwide—notably Loma Linda University and Medical Center; Battle Creek Sanitarium (Hospital) and Andrews University.

In 1888 the General Conference of Seventh-day Adventists convened. Fallout from this major event reverberates SDA ranks today, and laid foundation for Victor Houteff's message. The conference met in Minneapolis, Minnesota, October 17, 1888, preceded by a week long ministerial institute. Alonzo T. Jones and E.J. Waggoner, young co-editors for the <u>Signs of the Times,</u> a popular SDA periodical, presented a series of sermons on prophecy, and justification by faith.

Waggoner was also a medical doctor and minister. Both he and Jones held theological views that differed from contemporary SDA thinking. Their views on justification by faith and the law brought much opposition. The vast majority rejected it. (39, 40, 41) Mrs. White endorsed their message and views then and years later. "The message given by A.T. Jones and E.J. Waggoner," she wrote, "is the message of God to the Laodicean Church." (42)

To her and a few these were inspired messages from heaven. The general leadership rejected the message, ridiculed and mistreated the messengers. Because she supported Jones and Waggoner's pronouncements, Mrs. White was barbed also.

Of this embarrassing time for the denomination, Mrs. White wrote: "Never before have I seen among our people such firm self-complacency and unwillingness to accept and acknowledge light as was manifested at Minneapolis...They were actuated by the same spirit that inspired Korah, Dathan, and Abiram" [princes who rebelled against Moses in the Old Testament]. (43)

"The scenes which took place at this meeting made the God of heaven ashamed to call those who took part in them His brethren. All this the heavenly Watcher noticed, and it is written in the book of God's remembrance." (44)

Before this Conference of 1888, Mrs. White noted the unfortunate backsliding of the denomination as of 1882. "I am filled with sadness when I think of our condition as a people. The Lord has not closed heaven to us, but our own course of continual backsliding has separated us from God. Pride, covetousness, and love of the world have lived in the heart without fear of banishment or condemnation. Grievous and presumptuous sins have dwelt among us. And yet the general opinion is that the church is flourishing and that peace and spiritual prosperity are in all her borders.

"The church has turned back from following Christ her Leader and is steadily retreating toward Egypt." (45)

The 1880s and 1890s revealed that the church had lost much of its sincerity, charity, broad-mindedness, and humility of the 1830s and 1840s. According to critics, spiritual pride, hauteur, and confidence has grasped it by the throat.

After the 1888 meeting, Jones, Waggoner and Mrs. White traveled extensively, proclaiming this added knowledge. Some individual churches responded favorably, but most met it with indifference. The Foreign Missions Board invited Mrs. White to Australia. The trio disbanded and the message was doomed.

The aftermath of 1888, and the turn of the century led the church deeper into what some SDAs describe as "apostasy." Mrs. White and others called for revival and reformation (46)—a reorganization of the denomination. (47) Many SDAs believe that a feeble attempt was made in 1901, but the church was on a course out to sea that would leave it drifting without "chart or compass." (48)

Medical and educational institutions, conferences, all more and more moved away from the pioneers' blueprint. Adventism would never be the same again.

Chapter 4

When Men Shall Revile You

There is no pride like spiritual pride, no bigotry like religious bigotry. History is replete with atrocities that boggle the imagination and startle unbelievers. The irony is that these injustices, crimes, violence, wars were/are committed by religions espousing peace and equity.

We are forced to believe that more religious liberty and tolerance exists in the secular world than in the church—challenging paradox. Consider the persistent scourge of persecution in guise as religion. The pernicious belief that we have all truth and need nothing. Believe what we believe; teach what we teach or suffer the consequences. This type of religious zeal completely betrays and misrepresents true religion. It will bear responsibility for the blood of many wondering in skepticism.

One author regarded the church's role in society in the following way. "The state cannot teach morality or religion. It has not the credentials for it. The Spirit of God and the gospel of Christ are both essential to the teaching of morality, and neither of these is committed to the state, but both to the church.

"But though this work be committed to the church, even then there is not committed to the church the prerogative either to reward morality or to punish immorality. She beseeches, she entreats, she persuades men to be reconciled to God; she trains them in the principles and the practices of morality. It is hers by moral suasion or spiritual censures to preserve the purity and discipline of her membership. But hers it is not either to reward morality or to punish immorality. This pertains to God alone, because whether it be morality or immorality, it springs from the secret counsels of the heart; and as God alone knows the heart, He alone can measure either the merit or the guilt involved in any question of morals." (1)

In your search for true faith, do not let history discourage you. We are not without sterling examples of right. On one end there is a power that drives men to the depths of cruelty. On the opposite end there is a power that inspires men to the heights of love, bravery, integrity and dynamic faith. The former power leads to despotism and slavery of both body and spirit. The latter leads to freedom of soul, freedom of mind, and true serenity. Cruel men may enslave the mortal frame, but they cannot enslave those freed spirit.

Such were men and women burned at the stake; thrown into arenas and eaten alive by wild beasts; torn asunder; stretched on racks; speared through; tortured beyond imagination; boiled in oil; or seared with hot irons. Why? For a cause they believed in, and for which they were willing to die. For freedom to worship God according to the dictates of their own conscience.

Impure religious fervor sponsored the crusades. In its purity, it actuated the martyrs. The former was apostate Christianity. The latter was Christianity that embodied the words of its Founder. "Love your enemies, bless them that hate you, and pray for them which despitefully use you, and persecute you." (2) They crystallized true principles of right, true principles of God-like demeanor. They changed the world and overcame demons of bondage and persecution.

Seventh-day Adventists did not escape this two-sided phenomenon of persecution and unwavering faith. In 1888 when A.T. Jones and E.J. Waggoner presented their message, they were ridiculed and ostracized. Treatment which created schisms within the ranks of Adventism. Mrs. White sided with them and faced censure and opposition from many church officials angered by her pointed, stinging rebukes. These unholy actions by church officials indelibly stained the movement's history.

Similar events occurred with presentation of the Shepherd's Rod message. As the message permeated church ranks, opposition and hatred surfaced. Houteff and early believers reported the following incredible accounts.

"Indifference in this matter on the part of the laity has encouraged the leading brethren to exercise an imperious, cruel spirit by which they have brought disgrace upon the church of God. It caused us once even to be summoned before the city magistrate, and then afterwards, because the charges preferred against us failed to stand, thus depriving our accusers of the arm of the law with which to cast us out of the churches, it led them to take the reins in their own hands, and on four occasions bodily (on two of them violently) to carry some of us out of the church building. At another time it led them to have Brother Houteff arrested, but in vain, for the authorities, after questioning both sides found him guiltless, and ordered the same officers who took him to the police station to take him right back to the church where they picked him up, to the further humiliation and anger of his accusers. Then on another occasion, it stirred them to slap his face; and on still another, ruthlessly to batter his head and face until black and blue. After this latter attack, by a long time backslider whom they had stationed at the door as a watchman to keep us out, the prevailing sentiment of the multitude was, Perhaps now he will stay away!

"Then still later, this same spirit whipped them on so far that they tried to have him confined to a psychopathic ward, and failing in this also, then on even until they attempted to have him deported, again with no success but only greater humiliation and more ruthless anger to themselves...

"Then some time later, a brother who, being refused admittance to the church, was quietly standing at a window, listening to the lesson, had a glass of water dashed in his face from inside. On another occasion, at another S.D.A. church, this same brother, though being disabled, was simply because of his presence, savagely kicked (by one of the local elders) and knocked down in the rain and mud on the church sidewalk; while on still another occasion at a sister church and for the same reason, he was (by the minister this time) roughly jerked from his seat, where he had been sitting in perfect quiet, and bodily dragged from the church and plumped in a heap on the outer sidewalk! And these actions are but a sample of the many just like them taken by the church against brothers and sisters because of their desire to be better S.D.A.s. Yes, it is unbelievable, but it is true, nevertheless." (3)

Were perpetrators provoked or prodded into malevolence? No, by all accounts "Rod" adherents were generally well-respected members of their local churches and were engaged in normal church activities. The only reason for their mistreatment was their acceptance of the "Shepherd's Rod" message.

Obviously the "Rod's" message contained stern rebuke, placing denominational leaders and members in an unfavorable light. Like Mrs. White's testimonies, it spoke of the church's straying far from specific guidelines, standards, Biblical programs and principles established by church pioneers.

Much of the leadership no longer adhered to strict dietary practices. Adventists were counseled and encouraged to maintain specific hygienic rules. They were also encouraged in strict vegetarianism, avoiding all flesh foods. A well-balanced, lacto-ovo vegetarian regimen had been adopted by a majority by the turn of the century. By the 1930s, however, numerous church conference officials had regressed to meat eating, and were not particular about other dietary and hygienic guidelines.

The denomination's health facilities saw rapid, negative transformation from the original plan. Much of Mrs. White's counsel was ignored. Many considered it antiquated or impractical. Although she was not alive in the 1930s, her counsel on running the church's health institutions were explicit. Disastrous consequences would follow dishonoring divine counsel, placing the denomination's mission at risk.

Rather than constructing small facilities, keeping fees and services affordable even for the poor, the church built large facilities. Instead of focusing on prevention, natural hygiene and nutrition, avoiding usage of dangerous medications, they used allopathic medications almost exclusively. Services rose out of range for many. The denomination had patterned health care after the common order, and it became similar in operation. The way opened; in scurried financial aid and government intervention. With each change, they drifted further and further off course.

Years before the "Rod's" message came, Mrs. White commented. "There is danger that our college will be turned away from its original design. God's purpose has been made known—that our people should have an opportunity to study the sciences, and at the same time to learn the requirements of His word. Biblical lectures should be given; the study of the Scriptures should have the first place in our system of education.

"...But for one or two years past, there has been an effort to mold our school after other colleges. When this is done, we can give no encouragement to parents to send their children to Battle Creek College." (4) [Then headquarters of the denomination, brackets added.]

The denomination's educational institutions underwent similar transformation. Church leadership sought accreditation, which propelled its educational system into meeting secular requirements for recognition, another shift from the original plan.

Today, Loma Linda University and Loma Linda University Medical Center in Southern California; Andrews University in Berrien Springs, Michigan are accepted and praised as fine medical and educational institutions. By secular standards, they have done a good work. Most non-Adventists and a majority of Seventh-day Adventists respect them highly. However, a growing number of believers feel that they weave a fabric of apostasy. Thus, revealing that the church has failed to follow inspired guidelines. Thereby robbing the world of God given blessings.

Battle Creek Sanitarium (Hospital), in its early years under renowned surgeon, Dr. John Harvey Kellogg, was a prime example of what Adventist health reform should be. Agatha Thrash, MD summarized it this way: "One hundred years ago, in the day of Dr. John Harvey Kellogg, people from all over the world came to the Seventh-day Adventist sanitarium in Battle Creek. Many of these cases had been given up as hopeless—yet a surprisingly large proportion recovered at the sanitarium...Principally, the Battle Creek Sanitarium used enlightened diet therapy far in advance of that day, hydrotherapy, some manipulative therapy, along with the scientific use of all good medical procedures of the time. This therapeutic combination accomplished outstanding results with practically no harmful side effects. While some surgery was performed and some drugs administered, these treatments were rare compared to the carefully done physiotherapeutic procedures. The physicians were master physiologists, in far advance of physicians of later years." (5)

Had this unique program continued Battle Creek could have influenced medical practice on a large scale, perhaps throughout the 20th Century. Adherence to Mrs. White's counsel and Dr. Kellogg's skill forged Battle Creek Sanitarium ahead of its time. As observed, forward momentum in health reform did not last.

Houteff and associates were among the Adventists who recognized and acknowledged denominational health reform decadence. They viewed it as apostasy. Not only did the health institution's altered practices trouble them; the denomination's general mode of operation disturbed them also. Houteff addressed the situation, as he saw it, in a series of letters to the Elders and members:

"Truth challenges you, elders, to point out wherein the Bible teaches either by word or by example that the Sabbath and the church were made for raising goals, for auctioning, for selling literature and for taking subscriptions. The Bible does not teach or recommend even a plate collection (a custom which Rome originated) in Sabbath services, much less merchandising in the presence of God. All the Bible recommends is a container for freewill offering placed somewhere in the church premises. It was into such a treasury that the widow, while entering the temple, placed her two mites.

"You sell the Sabbath School quarterlies at a profit and then after studying the lessons you put the pressure upon the school members by which to squeeze every penny they may have with them. Following this they are again pressured into subscribing for magazines, periodicals, and then called upon to pay for church and school upkeep. Your high pressure and the laity's willingness to give, finally puts them in debt and makes them unable to pay their current bills! Thus you cause them to lose all the credit which a Christian, for Christ sake, deserves to have in the business world!

"And still worse, though the denomination takes away from the laity everything possible, she does nothing for them in time of need! But for you Elders she does everything that is to be done, although it is the laity who by hardship and sacrifice provide the means! Yes, you spend your last days in respect, comfort, and luxury, but when the laity get old and sick, or die empty-handed, you commit their cases to the world's charity institutions. What selfishness! What hardness of heart! What inequality and reproach against Christ!" (6)

"...Look and see what a difference there is between God's method for supporting His work, and the Roman system that is now carried on by the church; plate-passing, high powered speeches, Big Day, Book Day, high pressuring, campaigning, selling, auctioneering, Harvest Ingathering, birthday offerings, Christmas-tree hangings, baby weighings, Dorcas sales, investment funds, and what not! As none of these squeezings are Biblical, and as all of them are Pagan in origin and condemned by the Scriptures, they could not possibly be considered freewill offerings. Search and see.

"Instead of Sabbath-keeping the day is devoted to money raising, and instead of house of worship, the church is turned into a den of thieves—disgusting to observers, and most discouraging for a member to invite a friend or a neighbor to a church service...." (7) This frank and scalding description was not out of character for Houteff. He was known for his candor especially when involved in Spiritual matters or where he observed abuses or inequities. He was not alone; Mrs. White had mentioned similar sentiments. (8)

Houteff also believed the denomination ignored counsel in the area of salaried ministers. He believed pastors should not be paid a ministerial salary who did not work first to earn it.

"The plan of Christ forbids that any should enter the gospel ministry by salary...Consequently, both those who hire gospel workers by stipulated salary, and the ones who accept such a position are violating the Master's command.

"The present rule of the conferences is not only contrary to the Master's instructions but also responsible for not having 'many self-sacrificing workers,'...the conference demands all the tithe and offerings from the interest they develop.

"Thus any one who ventures to enter this sacred service is compelled to make his own way as long as he continues in the work, which does not only render the Lord's work impossible but also unfruitful for to keep up one's own expenses continually and feed a family besides will take most of one's time.

"It is neither Biblical nor just that one labor earnestly to raise up a company of believers, and then have the conference reap the tithe of his labor to feed a hired minister who had no part in the effort instead of the one who has sacrificed and done the work. Such an act might as well be called robbery." (9)

Houteff was not seeking to overthrow church leadership or form a new denomination. He sought a change or re-organization of the world-church, a return to what some SDAs termed primitive Godliness exemplified by the pioneers and protestant reformers. Houteff viewed himself as a reformer, and his message, God's Biblical voice to His people who had strayed from Him as an unfaithful wife committing a type of spiritual adultery. Houteff gave the message because he believed God had revealed it and had entrusted him with its proclamation. In these teachings rested hope for the church he admired. Houteff felt that he was constrained to speak out of deep devotion and love for God. Years after inception of his message he wrote:

"Like the early pioneers of the Adventist church, those who heed the Rod are the restorers of the 'old paths;' they realize the grave consequences involved in going contrary to any light the Lord chooses to send His people. And since the message of the Rod has aroused an interest in the need of 'reformation among God's people,' we as Davidians would not only be recreant to our trust but would also be passing 'by on the other side,' allowing our beloved Seventh-day Adventist church to drag in the dust, our brethren to be lost, and the world around us to perish for 'lack of knowledge,' if we did not bestir ourselves to warn the church of the oncoming danger." (10)

Houteff shared his beliefs with whomever listened. As mentioned previously, he taught them in his Sabbath school. As his Sabbath [Saturday] school expanded, he was forced to conduct Sabbath afternoon classes. As interest increased and the message spread, church leadership became defensive and angry. They tried again and again to halt Houteff's endeavors and convince him that his theological conclusions were, to say the least, misguided.

Around November 1929, J.E. Fulton, president of the Pacific Union Conference, and P.E. Broderson, president of the Southern California Conference, plus other conference officials and workers met with Houteff at Olympic Exposition Park Church. Houteff was grateful for the opportunity to present to them his message. What did they think of his views? One conference worker, Dr. W.G. Wirth said, "They were so fanciful that they did not take them seriously." (11)

But church members did take them seriously. Finally, by the spring of 1930, Houteff compiled his views in manuscript form entitled "The Shepherd's Rod." In May 1930, thirty-three hectographed copies were given to church leaders during the General Conference held in San Francisco, California, May 29—June 12, 1930. However, those who received the manuscripts failed to reply as requested.

SDA leadership tried vigorously to dissuade members from studying "The Shepherd's Rod." Anyone showing interest in investigating the "Rod" was denounced, and made an outcast. Physical abuse of "Rod" sympathizers sprouted in local churches like noxious weeds. Victims were stripped of their church positions if threats did not convince them to stop attending Houteff's meetings. Most yielded to the hierarchy's pressure, fearing loss of friends, of acceptance, and favor of their revered leaders. Only a courageous few followed their convictions openly. The "Rod's" Biblical expositions astonished and convinced. If unchecked, the message seemed destined to "leaven the whole."

On October 16, 1930, Conference leaders made another unsuccessful attempt to topple Houteff's theological position. In November of 1930, he published his first book entitled, "The Shepherd's Rod." Distributed to numerous denominational workers, it made its way throughout the conferences. In November of the same year, his local church voted to disfellowship (excommunicate) him. The motion, on November 20, was straight forward, it simply said:

"That for the protection of the church we withdraw the membership of Brother Houteff and our fellowship with him until such a time as he will conform to the church and withdraw his teachings." (12)

A larger rift emerged between those who embraced the "new" message and those who did not. Speaking many years later about the early days of the "Rod's" introduction, Houteff wrote: "Fundamentally, we are Seventh-day Adventists.

"...We are separated from the mother church because the 'lukewarm' brethren by majority vote disfellowshipped us, and put a guard at the church doors to make sure that we could not enter the churches on the Sabbath day. Evidently they did these things in order to force us to renounce the Lord's revealed Truth, and also to frighten those who were embracing Present Truth and those who might investigate for themselves and accept the message of the hour. There could be no other reason for dismissing us.

"...We have never, however, separated ourselves from the denomination. As a people we still attend the denominational churches whenever we are not barred from entering." (13)

Church leaders contend to this day that Houteff was stubborn, propagating his ideas persistently. "There was nothing left to do but disfellowship him."(14)

There is no question about his persistence or commitment to his beliefs. He believed, wholeheartedly, that what was revealed to him was not his message but God's. He was convinced that it had solid Bible support, not by choosing random texts, but was rooted in the Bible's framework. Most tried to dissuade him by using traditional thought, or teachings the church commonly accepted. Houteff took his hearers to task by showing that the fundamental teachings of Adventism were scripturally sound. But many of its traditional teachings, apart from these fundamentals, were not Biblically accurate. These traditional doctrines were borrowed from other writers and churches. Some practices were of pagan origin borrowed or accepted unwittingly from non-Biblical entities. They bear correction. Houteff constantly stressed that truth is progressive that the church is to advance in spiritual knowledge, and be a beacon to the secular world. In one of his later discourses he wrote:

"The same spirit prevailed in the Christian church. She never rose above the level on which the Apostles left her, and for a time she even fell almost to the bottom of the pit. And she would have dropped out had God not again visited His people in the persons of Luther, Knox, Wesley, Campbell, and the other reformers, through whom the Lord brought to light certain parts of Bible Truth that had long been trampled under foot. But did the Christian world as a whole see the light? And did all walk in it? No, indeed not, not as a people, but only as individuals. This is what accounts for the present multi-sectorial world; that is as it became necessary for Christ to organize a new church, the Christian, separate from the mother church, the Jewish, in His day, just so the reformers found themselves cast out from the mother churches, and necessarily were obliged to organize the followers of advancing truth into a new denomination, one after another.

"In this light, you see the spirit which keeps the Jews still Jews, the Buddhists still Buddhists, the Mohammedans still Mohammedans, the Catholics still Catholics, the Lutherans still Lutherans, the Methodists still Methodists, the Baptists still Baptists—the very same spirit is today working within our own denomination, the Seventh-day Adventists, presumptuously believing that they are rich and increased with goods, in need of nothing more." (15)

This was "non-progressive Christianity" (14) as he termed it. The denomination's handling of Houteff's case falls under question. First, can one be excommunicated lawfully for differing doctrinal beliefs, especially if they are not fundamental doctrines? Houteff insisted that he was a Seventh-day Adventist, accepting all basic, intrinsic beliefs of Adventism. A Seventh-day Adventist may be disfellowshipped (excommunicated) for flagrant moral indecencies or crimes, generally called, "open sin." However, Houteff was not guilty of moral misconduct.

Second, only two members supported the decision. According to the "SDA Church Manual," "members may be disfellowshipped or otherwise disciplined only by a majority vote of the members present and voting at a duly called meeting." (16) Some years after his severance from the local church, Houteff wrote:

"The news broadcast throughout the sisterhood of churches

and conferences, in both home and foreign fields, that the author of 'The Shepherd's Rod' is not a Seventh-day Adventist, is the blackest falsehood. I have been in good and regular standing, a believer of the advent truth in all its precepts without variation, from the day I first accepted the truth until now.

"Those who have read 'The Shepherd's Rod' will appreciate the fact that what I have stated is true. At the time the message of 'The Shepherd's Rod' came, I was both a member and officer in one of our churches. It was after the book had been written that my name was dropped from the church records by the church council with the support only of two lay members out of about 200; at which time our conference president said to me: 'I had to drop your name from the church records so that I can tell the churches that the book is not written by a Seventh-day Adventist.'

"Though our brethren think I am not now a Seventh-day Adventist, because they have (unlawfully) disregarded and deprived me my membership rights, how do they dare to say that 'The Shepherd's Rod' is not written by a S.D.A. when my name was still on the church books at the time the 'Rod' was written? And even now I am present to attend whenever possible the church where I had my membership at the time the message came, and similar is the case of each one who has connected with the message of the S. Rod." (17)

To Houteff this evidenced the church's political agenda. They feared proliferation of his message. In their perspective, he had to be discredited to lessen its influence. Should one be persecuted for variant theological views? Neither Houteff nor his supporters were found immoral, violent, or violators of proper Christian conduct. In fact, after accepting the new teaching, their conduct and lifestyles became even more commendable. Yet, other members engaging in blatant, questionable activities, were not excommunicated or disciplined. A fact known by many in the church today.

It is also known that doctrinal differences existed among the leadership then and now. Different pastors have preached substantially different views on a particular topic. Albeit, general harmony on fundamentals remained, but on certain peripheral subjects, discrepancies accrued. Precisely the "Rod's" case. It presented an alternate view on some peripheral subjects. Why did the denomination not accept the "Rod" as another theological option? The same question could apply to the 1888 Message. Preconceived opinions, and religious pride lay at the heart of the controversy. The fact that certain doctrines were taught one way for so long made it difficult for the leadership to consider objectively another point of view. It is, in fact, a human phenomenon.

Furthermore, the "Rod's" message demanded revival and reformation—a denominational reorganization of churches, hospitals, schools, and mode of operations. It was conservative in posture and pointed in delivery. Its stringency offended many. It was reformative—a stern, conservative message, a bold, challenging call. It did not put one at ease with the status quo. Adding insult to injury, it spoke of the church's judgment to come, because she failed to obey God's counsel. This judgment, as described in Ezekiel chapter nine, begins with five angels physically destroying the unfaithful in the denomination, commencing with the clergy. Unless one possessed an open-minded attitude and willingness to investigate reasons for the "Rod's" conclusions, he would reject it instinctively. This is in spite of the fact that Mrs. White encouraged objectivity. (18, 19) The Bible itself teaches that one should "prove all things; hold fast that which is good." (20)

In September, 1932, Houteff added a second volume to "The Shepherd's Rod," consisting of 304 pages. In 1933, he began writing a tract series. From 1932—1933 church leaders distributed rebuttals to the "Rod's" message. However, this did not stop the "Rod's" growth or influence.

These rebuttals attempted to show contradictions between Houteff's writings and Mrs. White's, but they did not refute his Biblical expositions point by point.
To the objective, unprejudiced mind, they did not offer sufficient evidence to reject the "Rod" believers. One could argue, then and now, that making two writers appear to contradict each other is not difficult. This tactic revolves in secular circles as well; without under-

standing the context of a writer's statement, it is easy work. All evidence showed that the church did not rebut the "Rod" on a biblical step-by-step basis but on the author's general statements; statements placed to appear that he contradicted Mrs. White. Although they approached some subjects from different angles, Houteff believed that the "Rod" fit in perfect harmony with her writings.

Believers point out that the compelling power of the "Rod" lay in its biblical base. While most church members lean heavily on Mrs. White's pen to explain difficult Biblical passages, Houteff allowed the Bible to explain itself. He referred to Mrs. White's writings for additional commentary. Although the denomination did believe in the Bible being its own expositor, it seemed to have neglected this principle in dealing with the "Rod." Adherents quickly referred to church founders for support, particularly Ellen White.

"Has not the same process been repeated in nearly every church calling itself Protestant?" says Mrs. White. "As its founders, those who possessed the true spirit of reform, pass away, their descendants come forward and 'new-model the cause.' While blindly clinging to the creed of their fathers and refusing to accept any truth in advance of what they saw the children of the reformers depart widely from their example of humility, self-denial, and renunciation of the world." (22)

In January 1934 the officers of the Fullerton, California, Tabernacle S.D.A. Church contacted the Pacific Union Conference requesting a hearing and official response to Houteff's message. The letter is important when studying the history of Davidian Seventh-day Adventists (DSDAs). It provides the agreement and protocol of what later some termed the infamous "unfair hearing." Quoting the letter in its entirety is necessary.

"To the Members of the Pacific Union Conf. Committee:

"Dear Brethren:
"We, as members of the Tabernacle Church of S.D.A. of Fullerton, Calif., after counseling with Victor T. Houteff concerning

the teachings of The Shepherd's Rod, respectfully request that you appoint a committee of ten or twelve 'brethren of experience' to meet with Brother Houteff while he places before them the evidence for his belief in the fundamentals of his message. The subjects to be considered are—'The Harvest,' 'Ezekiel 9,' 'The Leopard Beast of Rev. 13,' 'Hosea chapters 1-2,' and 'Matt. 20.' In these studies Brother Houteff is to use only the writings of the Bible and the Spirit of Prophecy.

"The time used is not to exceed one week.

"After each study the committee selected may retire for counsel, and may then submit its evidence for mistakes in Brother Houteff's teaching, such evidence to be drawn from the Bible and the Spirit of Prophecy only.

"If after the first study mistakes may be substantiated from authority mentioned above, further studies are not be given. The same conditions are to prevail after each succeeding study.

"In case the committee find error in the teaching of 'The Shepherd's Rod,' and are able to refute same by the Bible and the Spirit of Prophecy Brother Houteff agrees to denounce the advocacy of 'The Shepherd's Rod,' and to make public renunciation of same.

"Brother Houteff also agrees to discontinue the propagation of 'The Shepherd's Rod,' so far as he can control same, in the Pacific Union Conference, during the time this investigation is being made.

"The conditions hereby entered into are in compliance with the instruction given in 'Testimonies, Vol. 5,' page 293; 'Testimonies on Sabbath School Work,' pages 65-66."

Respectfully submitted,
Representatives for Tabernacle Ch.,
(signed) J.W. Rich
L. R. Sommerville

For 'The Shepherd's Rod'
(signed) V.T. Houteff (23)

Shortly after sending this letter to the Conference Mr. Rich wrote to Mr. Houteff, informing him that the Conference had agreed to "provide the committee that was requested in" the "arrangement;" "...that the Union [Conference] would try to get the men together within a couple of weeks for the hearing." Rich also stated that he did not know the personnel of the committee nor the time or place of their meeting. (24)

Houteff stated that he was contacted by two committee representatives about four weeks later. They informed him that the meeting would be held the following Monday. Because of a "pre-arranged, important engagement," Houteff and supporters requested a postponement. (24) He also received written confirmation from the Union Conference President, Glen Calkins of the meeting's proposed date and time. The same information he had received verbally but was obliged to postpone. Apparently the letter was in transit when he was verbally informed.

After learning of the committee make-up, Houteff detected a "set-up." In a letter to Mr. Calkins, dated February 15, 1934, he stated his concerns. Studying letters and historical accounts, it appeared that Houteff's concerns were justified.

"I am very glad for the opportunity that prompts me to write you this letter. Elder Prout has informed me that you have kindly agreed to respond to our request for a hearing.

"I am exceedingly happy to know of this agreement and shall be greatly delighted to present to such a committee the added light to the Third Angel's Message...

"When our appeal to the Union Conference was made by the members of the Tabernacle Church of Fullerton, California, and myself, it was verbally agreed that those who have been at war with 'The Shepherd's Rod' should be excluded from the committee, but Elder Prout's list of the proposed committee shows that nearly every one composing the personnel already is bitterly opposed.

"Realizing that we are dealing with a matter which involved our eternal interest, and of the destiny of our church members, the selection seems not only pernicious but also inadvisable for you to trust, and foolish for me to accept. For inasmuch as neither the General nor the Union Conference committees have acted upon the message of 'The Shepherd's Rod,' these men prove themselves unfit for the occasion, for they have heretofore acted independent of the conference—the highest authority—by speaking against the message from the pulpit and have even caused some of us to be carried bodily out of the church buildings for no other reason than our presence—shameful for the church of God! They, therefore, have already made the denomination liable for suit and heavy damages. Shall you let these men go further in their poor and despotic judgment? Moreover, they have published far and wide that I have been given a hearing by representatives of the denomination while they well knew that no such thing has taken place at any time!...

"I was further informed that I should appear alone before the committee. In this I see no wisdom at all. If the committee is to meet with me with the sole purpose to condemn and send one over the road, so to speak, regardless of justice or truth, and to rob God's church from a possible blessing in a message, then I say, it is wisely arranged. But I do not think this is your intention, Elder Calkins. I think you are honest to yourself and true to God." (25)

Houteff's pleas were ignored. He met with the committee on their terms. The meeting took place at the Hoover Street Tabernacle Church, Los Angeles, California on February 19, the stipulated date and time. The one exception, he did not meet with the committee alone. Records did not show who attended the meeting with Houteff. The basic terms, though, remained the same. He was to present the five subjects referred to in the Fullerton Tabernacle Church's letter of agreement. Houteff believed that he was forced into the meeting.

"Completely ignoring both our oral request and our written protest," said Houteff, "they uncompromisingly forced us into meeting them on their own terms. And so not to have wrung from our grasp the opportunity we had so long sought, and not to be made out as defaulters, to the detriment of the Truth, we were compelled to bow to their pleasure at our severe inconvenience, as well as to judges most of whom were already the 'Rod's' bitter enemies." (26)

Although most of the 12 man investigating committee were avowed opponents of the "Rod," it was a committee of some of the church's most respected leaders. Arthur G. Daniels was the committee chairman. Member make-up included, Glenn Calkins, Union Conference President; H.M.S. Richards (senior), distinguished speaker, and later founder of "The Voice of Prophecy Radio Ministry." These men wielded tremendous influence with church members. Other committee members were W.G. Wirth, secretary; G.A. Roberts, C.S. Prout, J.C. Stevens, C.M. Sorenson, F.C. Gilbert, W.M. Adams, J.A. Burden, and O.J. Graf.

Houteff was in a precarious situation. If the committee rejected his theological positions, he would lose credibility with church members. Labeling him a rebel, they would land a disastrous blow to the "Rod's" cause. If they accepted his positions, the message would gain enormous clout within the denomination. What was he to do if his message should be rejected? Should he submit to the leadership and recant? Could he conscientiously do so? Houteff was convinced that he was being railroaded. The entire cause was being placed on the altar. Echoes of 1888 must have sounded in his mind. If they had not heeded the Scripture's counsel or Mrs. White's counsel, whom they claimed to esteem, why would they accept his message?

The Greek Orthodox Church of his homeland had nearly taken his life. He was denounced, vilified, and forced to flee the country of his birth. Now Adventism placed him in similar circumstances. The church he loved and trusted; the people he called brothers and sisters in the faith, now treated him as a heretic. He and others had been physically assaulted and verbally abused. Now he stood before these church leaders, at their mercy, challenging their sense of fairness, justice, and moral integrity. Would they really give him a fair hearing? Would they give him an unbiased, objective investigation?

He prepared himself for the worst. Since 1928, he had proclaimed this special message. He had witnessed its convincing power, its efficacy in his own life and in the lives of countless others. His aspirations, his hopes, his spirituality, and his faith had deepened and broadened. He felt wrapped in the love of God. Not he alone, but so many others had witnessed and experienced the potent, sweet influence of divine revelation through the medium of this message, "The

Shepherd's Rod." To them the Bible lived, not as a book of fables, nor as mythological intrigue, but as the word of God.

How could he turn his back on all that to please men, no matter how prominent? Houteff determined to give the truth and leave the results with God. It was right that the leadership hear the message formally, although, he knew their minds were already made up. This hearing was only a ploy to further discredit him and to beguile the laity. However, he could not, and would not turn back. He would only retreat, if the committee found clear Biblical evidence to refute the message.

At 10:30 a.m., Houteff proceeded with his presentation of the subject of "The Harvest" and continued for about two hours. At the close of his discourse, the chairman, A.G. Daniels suggested that after lunch he continue with another discourse. Houteff kindly requested that instead they deliberate on what they had already heard, returning with a decision as to whether the presentation was, in their opinion, erroneous or correct. This, he urged, was part of the written agreement. Daniels disagreed and pressed to have him go on with his next study. "We have brought these men here from far away," Daniels replied. "They are ready to stay two days, three days, a week or two weeks, however long it is necessary for us to get the full picture in our minds..." (27) Houteff again urged them to deliberate on what they had already heard before moving on, according to the agreement.

What apparently was on Houteff's mind was the agreement formulated by the Fullerton Tabernacle Church specifically elucidated the terms of the meeting. It listed the five subjects for Houteff to present. The first being "The Harvest," then "Ezekiel Nine," etc. It stated, "The time is not to exceed one week. After each study the committee selected may retire for counsel, and may then submit its evidence for mistakes in brother Houteff's teachings..." (28)

J.W. Rich's letter to Houteff, after the agreement was sent to the Conference, confirmed that the Conference committee had accepted it. That along with the conference's other contacts with Houteff showed clearly that they agreed to the arrangement. Now, in the midst of the proceedings, they changed the agreed upon protocol.

Houteff felt his best course was to stay with the original plan. He was not deterred although he was asked repeatedly to proceed. "If you cannot agree with the first, why continue," he responded. Finally, Daniels closed the meeting, stating that they needed time to deliberate and research Houteff's discourse on "The Harvest." The meeting adjourned with the understanding that they would respond to "The Harvest" study alone. (27, 29)

The committee responded to Houteff's presentation in about four weeks instead of the specified one week time frame. (30) On March 18, the committee met with Houteff and twelve "Rod" adherents, and read their findings. The report they subsequently entitled, "Reply to the Shepherd's Rod." Apparently Houteff and "Rod" supporters were not allowed to respond in the meeting for he later stated:

"Immediately after reading it to us, they adjourned the meeting inflexibly denying our insistent plea for even three minutes time in which to make a statement." (30) There is no documented denial of this by the denomination. Commenting further, Houteff said:

"Such arbitrary and inconsiderate proceedings, anything but Christ-like, indicate that the committee well knew that their report against the "Rod" had not refuted a single point. For had they believed otherwise, they right there and then would have solemnly charged us to honor our agreement to retract our teachings, and would then have thrown the meeting open for testimonies of confession. But no, they refused to hear a word from any of us!" (30)

Another point of interest, the committee did not respond to "The Harvest" study alone as stipulated. Instead, they addressed the entire message, deriving their information from his books or other written sources concerning his teachings.

All this riveted in Houteff's mind that denominational leaders had no intentions of fair dealing with him. But they had established the committee as a political ploy to discredit him and his work. They were looking for an "out," a way to convince the laity that they had objectively dealt with "The Shepherd's Rod." They banked on the fact that, in religious circles, most lay members accepted without question what their clergy or leaders taught them. Houteff knew most members would ask, "Did our leaders investigate 'The Rod'?" "Has Elder Richards accepted the message?" "What does Elder Daniels think of this 'Shepherd's Rod' business?"

The answer was academic. At that juncture, Houteff's writings would be trashed, and his character impugned. The author has witnessed these types of questions and responses numerous times. It is amazing to see someone emphatically reject something knowing little or nothing about it. This repetitive history of behavior seemed to substantiate Houteff's concern about the committee's true motives.

In fact, Houteff and "Rod" adherents were not surprised by the situation. Anticipating the conference committee's unfair performance, several "Rod" believers formed an advisory committee and adopted certain resolutions. The resolutions were adopted in Los Angeles, California, on March 12, 1934. Approximately six days prior to the conference committee's verbal report to Houteff.

The "Rod's" advisory committee's resolutions were not publicized until after the conference committee had given their report. It opened a window on "Rod" believers concerns and how they related to the denomination. Again it is important to quote the exact words.

"Therefore, as a united body of believers in the message of Present Truth, as contained in the publications of the 'Shepherd's Rod' (which we believe have come in response to divine enlightenment, and are the 'unrolling of the scroll' (5), in perfect harmony with the Third Angel's Message as set forth in the Bible and Testimonies for the Church, we herewith declare:

"Be it resolved, that we direct our full support to the proclamation of Present Truth, in harmony with the S.D.A. doctrines as originally given through the Bible and the Testimonies; but that we respectfully protest against the actions of our brethren in disfellowshipping and excluding members from the churches which they have helped to build up, simply because they exercise their God-given rights in making a personal investigation of purported new light (6); and "the fact that there can be no new organization, clearly shows that all our work must be done in and for our S.D.A. church. We trust, therefore, that our desire to worship in the church of our choice, even though we have by her been deprived of our membership (and that for no other reason than for accepting 'more light' on the Third Angel's Message) (17), will not be denied, and that our presence will not be forbidden." (31, 32)

Questions arose regarding how the conference committee arrived at its report, and how they treated Houteff after its issuance. One conference committee member, H.M.S. Richards (senior), after being asked for specific errors he saw in Houteff's message, reportedly said, "The brethren [the remainder of the committee] said they found error in it." (33)

Evidently, the report's phraseology and argument was that of Professor O.J. Graf, more evidence to "Rod" adherents that the response was slanted to the theological preconceptions of one mind as opposed to twelve. It indicated to them that the conference committee had prejudged the message. Obviously, they had delegated composition of their preconceptions to Professor Graf. The report was then read and accepted as the committee's official position. Hence, individual members executed exemption from personal, objective research.

As mentioned earlier, the booklet containing the committee's findings was entitled, "A Reply to the Shepherd's Rod." With its publication the denomination hoped to defuse a theological time-bomb. The General Conference paddy-backed the Pacific Union Conference's (the committee of 12's) work.

On April 16, a special committee was appointed by the General Conference to publish a pamphlet entitled "A Warning Against Error." On May 8, 1934, the General Conference commissioned a new committee to re-examine "A Reply to the Shepherd's Rod." By May 14, this re-examination was approved by the General Conference.

All rebuttals contained the same information and have taken the same fundamental approach. They basically compared, often out of context, selected statements from Houteff with selected statements from Mrs. White—a strategy used in religious and political circles; methods accepted as unreliable and sometimes blatantly dishonest by, what Davidians term, fair-minded people. The denomination never has addressed the "Rod" on a point by point Biblical basis.

Furthermore, some teachings they condemned Houteff for they published themselves before and after the 1934 hearing. For example, Houteff wrote:

"As the wounded head has reference to the stroke delivered to the Papacy by Luther, the exile of the Pope in 1798 was a sign of the completeness of the wound and the prophetic period ended...but the blow weakened his power, and the result was that Protestantism came upon the stage of action. The continual infliction began to irritate the 'head' until finally the Pope landed behind prison bars." (34)

In 1934 in one of its foremost publications, the denomination wrote:

"The 'deadly wound' here forecast found its fulfillment in the protestant reformation, in the French revolution and culminated in the apparently mortal thrust at the very heart of the papacy when the pope was deposed and imprisoned by the French in 1798." (35)

Both statements are substantively the same. The denomination generally held that the deposing of Pope Pius VI in 1798 was the fulfillment of the Biblical reference found in Revelation 13:3. It speaks of the wounding of a seven-headed, ten-horned, leopard-like beast. Houteff believed that the infliction of the wound was a process which began with Martin Luther's protest, which developed into the Protestant Reformation and climaxed in 1798. Although the church's own publication expressed an almost identical position as Houteff's, he was severely rebuked and persecuted for it. The same holds true for the "Rod's" teachings on other subjects.

Houteff did not detour from his work. He was driven forward to declare what he believed. Shortly after the infamous meeting, Houteff formed The Universal Publishing Association. It became the primary means of publishing and distributing his literature.

Neither did the church cease her resistance.

"Rod" believers were verbally and physically assaulted regularly—knee-jerk behavior continuing to this day. Ridicule, scorn, malicious rumors, and malignity of all sorts hound many "Rod" believers world-wide.

To know the true purpose, work and message of "The Shepherd's Rod," one must study it. Asking the average Seventh-day Adventist for an unbiased opinion of the "Rod" is like asking Republicans for unbiased opinions of Democrats. Or for Palestinians to give unbiased judgment on the State of Israel.

In one of his last publications, entitled, "The Whitehouse Recruiter," Houteff encapsuled the entire incredible situation. "Do not, though, let anyone fool you into believing that the 'Recruiter' is calling you out of the Seventh-day Adventist denomination and into something else....

"By having instilled in rank and file throughout Laodicea an unprecedented fear and prejudice against reading or hearing anything but that which enjoys someone's official sanction and blessing. Satan's subversives have sought to sever the lines of communication between the Spirit of Truth and the people of God. Then to hold them in subjection to themselves and their worldly standards, they threaten with disfellowshipment and perdition any who, fearing God more than man, would dare venture to know the Truth for themselves. And the few who do have the courage to carry out their convictions, straightway in consequence become targets for the Enemy's fiercest darts of opposition, bitterest prejudice, scandalizing falsehood and character defamation, ridicule and scorn and hatred, embarrassment and hardship. Thus 'all that will live godly in Christ Jesus' (2 Tim. 3:12) find themselves 'outcasts' (Isa. 66:5; Luke 6:22; Acts 24:14) at the hands of persecutive forces perpetuating and even outdoing the worst that was ever in Judaism and Romanism. And what is still worse, when these revivalists of tyranny, clothed in apostle like robes, succeed in confusing and overthrowing the faith of an investigator or of a follower of Truth for this very time, they compel him to submit to rebaptism in order to be readmitted into church fellowship, even though he has become more faithful than ever before! What astounding blasphemy!" (36)

On another page he wrote: "But as the church today is virtually everywhere in subordination to the state, and therefore utterly powerless to impose the penalty of imprisonment, torture, and death, as her predecessors frequently did, in punishment for supposed heresy, the threat of excommunication is consequently the highest price that the denomination is able to impose upon any who would dare to awaken her sleepers. Likewise it is become her strongest weapon for persuading the awakened to retract and to lapse back into Laodicean slumber and sleep."

The denomination does not place "Rod" believers in positions of responsibility (at least not knowingly). That may not raise objection, but abuse and ostracism is unacceptable by any standard. Yes, even today the name, "Shepherd's Rod," conjures inexplicable fear, loathing, or passionate cruelty—witnessed over and over again by many, including the author.

Dedicated "Rod" believers pressed down, almost beyond measure; overwhelmed with the enormity of their task; a task they undertake with inordinate zeal. They walk a path few would dare travel. They continue to declare what to them is a truth that burns within their souls, to a people who treat them as virulent pests. It is sometimes difficult for an outsider to grasp.

"Why not leave them alone?" One may ask. "We can not!" Would be a true Davidian's reply. "We dare not refuse to publish the message. Love demands it." They take comfort in the words of Christ.

"Blessed are they which are persecuted for righteousness sake, for theirs is the kingdom of heaven. Blessed are ye, when men shall revile you, and persecute you, and shall say all manner of evil against you falsely, for my sake. Rejoice, and be exceeding glad, for great is your reward in heaven for so persecuted they the prophets which were before you" (Matt. 5:10-12).

Chapter 5

Building Mt. Carmel Center—Waco, Texas

Establishment, and climax of Mt. Carmel Center, Waco, Texas, encompassed the best and worst of the DSDA experience. From this location, literature traveled to homes, hands, laps, pockets, yards, or waste baskets by the millions throughout the SDA world. The message denominational leaders sought to crush shook Adventism at its core.

At Mt. Carmel Center, Davidians could have realized their fondest hopes, joys, and greatest expectations. Instead, they tasted the gaul-laden cup of disappointment. This bitter draft was not the death of Davidia, but it was sort of a knockout blow, creating temporary disorientation. Davidia survives today with its name and work tarnished by detractors, splinter groups, and pseudo representatives teaching doctrines, espousing ideas contrary to Houteff's message. One such individual was Vernon Howell known to the world as David Koresh. The names "Waco, Texas," and "Mt. Carmel Center" became infamous during a Federal raid on the Branch Davidian headquarters near Waco and its history-making aftermath.

The name "Mt. Carmel" springs from an ancient hill where the Israelite prophet, Elijah, reclaimed back-slidden Israel from religious apostasy. An outstanding victory in Israel's history; it saved almost the entire nation from wholesale idolatry. (1)

Carmel also symbolized rich, green, spiritual pasture for the flock—an analogy used in Scripture by the Old Testament prophets, Micah and Amos. Both the "Shepherd's rod," and "Carmel" were used symbolically by Micah. His sixth chapter speaks of hearing the "rod." Chapter seven speaks of feeding the flock (the church) with the "rod" in three lush pastures of which "Carmel" is the first. Obviously Micah was not referring to a literal shepherd's staff. Mt. Carmel represented a place where one could acquire an abundance of spiritual knowledge to feed the soul. The shepherd's rod symbolized that food.

Houteff stated that he was unaware of these texts when he named his first book, "The Shepherd's Rod," and named the center, "Mt. Carmel." In an article addressed to one denominational leader, Houteff declared:

"It might be interesting to Elder G. to know that the naming of our "camp" "Mt. Carmel Center" came about in the same way as the naming of our publications, "The Shepherd's Rod," for we did not know before hand that it was in prophecy until after our attention was called to Micah 7:14 and Amos 1:2." (2)

This chapter traces the roots, events, and progress of the original Mt. Carmel Center which bore no resemblance to the Branch Davidian Association headquarters either in nature or location.

Although Houteff and early pioneers of the Davidian movement felt compelled to establish an association to disseminate their message, it was a difficult step for many. To a majority of church constituents it appeared that Houteff was launching another denomination. He explained repeatedly that it was not a separate denomination but a ministry—an independent ministry. In fact, Houteff forbade establishment of another world church. To some, the apparent separation erected a fearful barrier. Numerous SDAs agreed with the message, but could not openly support the Association. Houteff and pioneers felt that they could not do otherwise since denominational leaders denied them free expression. These convictions were confirmed regularly by consistent physical and verbal harassment against those who dared embrace the "Shepherd's Rod" teachings.

Time has somewhat diluted the constituency's fear of establishing ministries independent of church hierarchy. Today, about 800 independent ministries exist within SDA borders. (3) Most are not under denomination authority, and many are denounced by church leadership. This polarization profoundly affects the organized work. As church leaders exercise more and more intolerance and continue demanding explicit homage, the rift widens and places the church in a financial, theological, and organizational dilemma. In an effort to uproot what it sees as unfair competition, the denomination has stooped to prosecuting some of these ministries. (4)

Knowingly or unknowingly a few of them have embraced and are teaching part of "The Shepherd's Rod." Today, the church is confronted with similar circumstances as when it attempted repudiating the "Rod" in the 1930s. She has not escaped the inevitable. Her denunciation of the "Rod" was the push that birthed more children, who have come of age to reckon with what some Adventists consider their unfaithful mother. Yet Davidians, even to many of these independent movements, are a radical older brother from whom they prefer keeping a safe distance lest they too be condemned.

When Houteff and associates formed the Universal Publishing Association in Los Angeles, California in 1934, it signified a new formality in his work. It established a self-supporting movement within Adventism focused on distributing a controversial message. Besides the first two volumes, he published pocket-sized booklets or tracts. This allowed ready reading access since they could be carried easily while traveling. In a short time, these tracts penetrated the thick walls of church opposition and prejudice.

The publishing ministry afforded an immediate, unpressured, uncensored avenue, reaching parishioners while protecting privacy. Curious people wondered what caused the fuss that had their leaders seething with anger. Why were they pursuing Houteff? Why were they intent on preventing individual investigation of his claims? "There must be something to it!" Some exclaimed. As one would study these expositions, he was usually astounded. Convinced of their Biblical veracity, he would share them with others. The leaders' intensified denunciations only watered newly planted seeds of conviction. Church members realized the leadership's inability to substantially refute Houteff's claims on a Biblical basis. Their hatred and violence drove many toward the "Rod."

The majority of Seventh-day Adventists feared recrimination and isolation too much to brave investigation. However a large class was pulled by the "Rod's" magnetic attraction. If the SDA clergy believed the "Rod" was as dangerous as fire to their parishioners, they unwittingly chased them into the flames.

The growth of the movement can be illustrated by the publishing work. For example, the first printing of the two "Shepherd's Rod" volumes (1930 and 1932)—about 5,000 copies each. Early printing of his first and second tracts in 1933—about 3,000 copies. (5) In 1934, when he published the third and fourth tracts, the numbers increased slightly. He printed 5,000 copies of tract three and 6,000 of tract four. (5)

By the 1940s, he completed a fifteen tract series; each booklet comprised 50 to 118 pages. He added a five volume answer book series; several separate booklets; hundreds of articles in the Association's official magazine, "The Symbolic Code;" and 98 smaller booklets, "Timely Greetings," containing sermons. His writings were distributed by the millions. (6, 7) At the time of his death in 1955, after 25 years of work, he had completed about 15,000 pages of difficult theological, Biblical expositions, and written hundreds of letters. His literature touched nearly every continent and country housing Adventists, including China.

Here is an intriguing story of a couple living in 1946 China, and how they came in contact with the "Rod." The account was related in a letter to the Association.

"I picked up half of your booklet [Tract #13] on the street, and my wife a few days later picked up the other half beside the curb of the same drive. I pieced them together, and got your address. I am deeply interested in all it contains, and am anxiously waiting to hear from you. Could you tell me everything that will help me find my joy?" (8)

"The Shepherd's Rod" shook the SDA denomination. Millions of booklets were posted to both clergy and laity throughout the Adventist world. Most received them with dismay or contempt. Many did not read them but disposed of them via stove, waste basket, or fireplace. Nevertheless, by 1955 there were about 100,000 Adventists on the regular mailing list. (9) Those who read the materials and showed signs of more than casual interest numbered about one tenth of the denomination's membership. It is believed that almost twice that number accepted some of the message but had not committed to the Association or its overall work. (10)

Thus, what Adventist leadership tried to squash in its infancy had mushroomed into an established entity. What enabled the movement to spread and become grafted into the tree of Adventism? The formation of Mt. Carmel Center. Houteff and "Rod" pioneers realized the point of no return. They recognized the need of a base of operations. Since the SDA denomination denied "Rod" believers all church privileges, a central headquarters was needed from which to print and distribute literature. There they could provide homes for the aged and infirm; train workers in theology; in basic trades; in nutrition and health. Knowledge of health care was vital, because in most cases believers were refused service at Adventist hospitals.

Their children were not accepted into Adventist schools. Their elderly were refused admittance to SDA rest homes. Even though many "Rod" believers contributed time and funds to their local churches and conferences, they were denied financial aid from the denomination. While this was not true in all cases, it happened often enough to raise more than casual concern. An announcement placed in the Association's newsletter, August 1934, described the situation.

"Being deprived of all denominational advantages such as sanitariums [hospitals], health food factories, printing presses, etc., perhaps it may be necessary for a rural location for the establishment of a combined unit to assist in carrying the message to the church...This has been suggested by a sister and her husband who have had considerable experience in this line. Therefore we call the attention of all who are standing in the light to give consideration to such a location and the necessary information regarding it..." (11) After considering this suggestion, the "Rod" leadership decided on Texas.

The opening of the 20th Century found Texas with a sound economy. Discovery of oil and the subsequent oil boom enhanced its economic make-up, bringing wealth to the state. Commerce and industry blossomed, cities grew under its rising star. As with the rest of the country, during the 1930's depression, it saw sharp drops in business and industry. However, the 1930s also introduced new programs which swung the state back into an economic upturn. Texas was an ideal spot to establish a center.

Perhaps, at that time, its geographical location was the most important reason early Davidians chose Texas. Centrally situated between the Americas, Texas facilitated easier access to the largest concentration of Adventists perched primarily in North, Central, and South America. In 1934 and 1935, Adventists numbered approximately 400,000 worldwide. The majority resided in the western hemisphere—the Americas. Hence, housing the Davidian headquarters in Texas would produce ready access to them.

In February, 1935, Houteff and two believers, M.L. Deeter, and E.T. Wilson (a former SDA conference president) met in San Antonio, Texas, to locate an ideal spot for the future headquarters. (12) Believing that God had led them to this vicinity, their search circled San Antonio, Fort Worth, and Dallas. (12) How could they build a center of lofty ideals amidst a national depression? How could so few with so little launch such an arduous endeavor? They needed a self contained area capable of housing hundreds of workers. It must accommodate a bustling publishing facility, rest home, schools, Bible institute, offices, and a huge kitchen to feed residents. Such a site had to be rural with abundant acreage.

"One thing was clear in our minds concerning the new home for our work," said Houteff, writing in 1935, "and that was that we should have a rural base from which to operate." (12)

For two months, they pursued every possibility. In Waco, attention focused on a property approximately five miles from the heart of town. Situated near Lake Waco—an artificial lake which provided the city's water supply, and about a mile of highway frontage. Today that highway is known as Highway 6—Lake Shore Drive. The natural, rustic setting rendered it a picturesque location.

The property comprised 189 acres, half in timber—cedar, oak, elm—half in cultivatable land. From the lake side rose a rapid incline about 300 feet possibly the highest point in Waco. Except for two canyons dividing the woods into two hilltop sections, the land was relatively level, excellent for building. (12) The three site-hunters were impressed; this would be the center's future home. It was summed up this way:

"...So the more we considered this location the more convinced we were that the Lord was directing us to this place, as evidenced by many infallible proofs, which we dare not question, for the whole setting of the scene was at first contrary to any human planning of our own." (12)

Waco lies about 90 mile south of Dallas/Fort Worth, and about 180 miles northwest of Houston in McClennan County, about 427 feet above sea level. Waco was established in 1849 on the ancient settlement of the Huaco Indians. In 1542, the Spanish explorer, Luis De Moscosco DeAlva-Rado traveled across northeast and central Texas. He was the first to map the location of the Waco village, situated close to the confluence of the Bosque and Brazos Rivers.

In 1934, Waco was not the bustling city of over 3,000,000 that it is today. Its 100 miles of trade territory make it a leader in transportation, banking, industry, agriculture, and recreation. In the 1930s it was a farm town. No one could have imagined the future impact of that 189 acre purchase nor of the unique campus it would raise by what appeared then as an unwanted, obscure people.

On May 24, 1935, eleven believers and Houteff arrived from California to establish the center. (13) A few of the twelve pioneers resided in Waco; the remainder camped on the hill, working the untamed land into living quarters. Months of difficult labor and trying circumstances lurked ahead, but the official move from Southern California had begun.

They had no well or water, no roads, no buildings, no electricity. They had nothing but earth, trees, rocks, and sky. Office buildings, living quarters, laundry, kitchen, dining area, classrooms, and a chapel could have been constructed in a matter of months with sufficient capital, skilled crews, and modern equipment.

Mired amidst a severe national depression, these pioneers had no such advantages. They possessed no excavating equipment, scant capital, and at first had no skilled builders or craftsman among them. Oliver Hermanson, one of the twelve who later became Houteff's brother-in-law, described those early days:

"There was nothing on the place but timber and brush. The

ax was the first tool to go into use. Construction first began on a simple flat roof frame building to house the institution's and the pioneers belongings that were to be brought by trucks a few days after the group of twelve arrived. The builders at first slept and cooked in the open under the trees. Black gumbo muddy roads to walk and drive over, water to be had only by hauling a distance of six miles in barrels the first two years, and later in a 300 gallon tank, kerosene lamps for light, poor housing and home-made wood stoves were a few of the obstacles that faced the pioneers." (14)

Making bad matters worse, these settlers—nine adults, one teenager, two children—were in poor health. Said Houteff:

"...It was found among our governmental number...that we were not only poor but also badly crippled. Four of us have the use of one hand only—two with permanent injury—besides other deformities and afflictions over the entire caravan." (15)

The following list highlights the twelve zealous pioneers. E.T. Wilson; Mr. and Mrs. Charboneau, her daughter, Sopha Delle Hermanson; Mrs. Hermanson's son and daughter, Oliver and Florence; Mr. and Mrs. J. Berolinger; Mr. M.L. Deeter and his daughter, Naoma; Mr. John Knippel Sr.; and Victor Houteff.

Mr. E.T. Wilson was a former SDA conference president and early "Rod" believer. He lost his administrative position and ministerial credentials because of his open stand for the "Rod." Wilson worked closely with Houteff throughout those turbulent, early years. He became vice president of the Davidian Association, respected for his fervor and spirituality.

Mrs. Florence Floretta Chaboneau, wife of Charles Charboneau (a non-SDA), mother of Sopha Hermanson was the highly respected first active convert to Houteff's message. After church leaders ousted Houteff's class, her home across from the church served as their meeting place on Sabbath afternoons. She was the Association's first treasurer. (16)

She arrived in Texas with the first group. Her dwelling was the first home erected. Six months after arrival, she was the first to pass away among the believers and the first buried in Mt. Carmel's cemetery. She had held a special place in Houteff's heart. Speaking at her funeral, he stated, "Ever since I met our dear sister about ten years ago I have found her to be one of the most faithful servants of God I have ever met. Her faith I have never seen waiver. She has always stood steadfast for the message we bear ever since it came and has sought to promote its advancement even beyond her strength and has never held back from helping others." (16)

Mrs. Charboneau died December 2, 1935, ten days before her 62nd birthday. Until completion of her new home, she had resided in Waco. Though in poor health she had served as Association treasurer until her passing. Although today, the city limits has engulfed the entire area, and the Center no longer exists, the street named after her still remains.

Mrs. Sopha Hermanson, Mrs. Charboneau's daughter, became treasurer and held office for many years. Victor Houteff married her daughter, Florence Hermanson. Florence was a teenager, between 15 and 17 years old, when she arrived in Texas with her mother, younger brother, Oliver, and grandparents. Unknown to them, she and Oliver were destined to play key roles in the future of Davidia.

The group's zeal was undampened by the enormous task facing them. They felt that more than human power guided their affairs. Their ardent faith met challenge after challenge. Young and old alike dug foundations, hammered, sawed, mixed cement and mortar, and prepared meals in primitive conditions. Amidst poisonous snakes and oppressive Texas heat, they labored long and rested little. Kerosene lamps and a gasoline-powered generator provided light and electricity. They hauled water in from Waco.

Extravagance was not a consideration. Pitted against the "very, very short" time they anticipated being there, elaborate buildings were impractical. (2) Simplicity was wisdom's choice. They firmly believed in simplicity with quality.

The Center's objective was not to establish a commune or gathering place, but to establish a base of operations. From this international headquarters, the Davidian leadership would coordinate a worldwide network of believers. Houteff described the Center's purpose this way:

"...Mt. Carmel Center is being built as a base of operation for training and fitting workers to carry this special message to the church; for educating deserving youth; for caring for worthy poor, aged, widowed, and orphaned; and for ministering to the sick and infirm according to God's plan." (17)

How would they reach their goal—the Center's completion, with limited funds, time, and hands? How would Mt. Carmel Center become a point of impact to the church and society? These questions pelted their minds like the relentless Texas sun which blistered their bodies. Every stroke of the hammer; every push and pull of the saw; every swing of the ax tried their faith, contested their hopes.

Was it possible that they were deluded enthusiasts—simpletons caught unawares in a cunning web of deception spun by some clever charlatan spider? Was Houteff all he appeared to be—earnest, caring, gifted, a man called of God, a messenger for the time? Or, was he that charlatan spider? They had forsakened everything for the cause. Reputations—dearest dreams—dearest aspirations—future plans. Their lives were spread on the sacrificial altar, under time's inevitable knife.

Although their physical vision was often blinded by a blazing sun, they saw a greater light. Each day birthed arduous labor under overwhelming odds. With each blow of the hammer, with each stroke of the ax or saw, a strength beyond their own urged them on. They worked, confident that a power beyond themselves, beyond Houteff, beyond the denomination, directed their steps. They felt constrained by Biblical evidence; by the hope of God's promises; by a sweet message giving them a glimpse of glory; by an inner peace that had changed their lives completely.

Those pioneers would soon see their faith rewarded as they made slow but steady progress. Each month brought believers from various locations nationwide to build the camp. By summer's end, the hill's population had blossomed from twelve to approximately 37. Some resided in Waco for lack of housing on the hill. Contented hearts willing to bear one another's load, they demonstrated genuine love and comradery. (18)

As time passed, skilled tradesmen arrived boosting camp building. By August, 1935, they had partially completed two frame structures. One was a warehouse, sleeping quarters, kitchen, dining room combination. There they conducted morning and evening devotions, but its primary use was kitchen and dining room. The second building was used for living quarters only. (18) By October, an office building and additional living quarters were erected. The training school's foundation was laid. Though incomplete, all buildings were usable. However, they lacked running water and city electricity.

By 1936, they added a windmill that pumped water up hill to a large water tower and furnished much of the camp's water supply. The well-house was a small shack atop a cistern. (10) Total acreage rose in October that year to 375 with acquisition of 186 acres. This unpopular purchase later evolved into an asset.

In 1938, electricity arrived from Waco, illuminating the several, almost completed buildings. A dairy farm with 12-15 cows and 30-40 goats, large apiary, small chicken farm, sawmill, vegetable farm, mercantile, dispensary, printshop, peach orchard, offices, and chapel graced the grounds.

1939 produced public lavatories, showers, and other improvements. The Center had two dams. One partially completed, the other called Lake Meribah, became excellent source for much of the camp's water supply.

By 1942, the Center consisted of six main buildings and a number of subsidiary structures. Five were of frame and stone construction. Native Austin rock, clay, and cement, excavated by camp residents was also used. These supported administrative offices, chapel, classrooms, dormitories, other living quarters, kitchen, dining room, laundry, dispensary, nursery, storage shed, pump-house, water tower, water-works control house, and produce depot.

Building eight was perhaps the most interesting, it held the center's heart. There resided administrative offices, publishing office, and mercantile. Its second story housed the general assembly hall or chapel, plus apartments. Houteff lived in one, having a small living room, kitchenette, and bedroom.

Made into the very masonry of the ground floor was a huge pictorial clock, its arms pointing just before 11 o'clock. To an outsider, it presented an arresting, odd, perhaps mysterious face. To an Adventist, it announced the approach of the 11th hour; the last hour of earth's history; the end of the present order of things.

In many ways, the llth hour theme crystallized the Davidian message. It climaxed their prophetic graph of earth's history. It met the apocalyptic junction of hope, faith, joy of the heavenly-minded, past and present—mingled with the worst of mankind who will face the judgment of an omnipotent God.

Most of what was Mt. Carmel is gone, but this building with its ominous timepiece is still used, today. Perhaps that clock reminds present occupants of those who gave their all preparing a people to meet the last days of our present world. Perhaps it is still a subtle reminder of the world's approaching the 11th hour. Or, does it invoke innate skepticism of religion—another example of man's vulnerability to quixotic quests? Whatever one's conclusion, when all else fails, time will not fail to inscribe the truth on its stony pages.

The campus neared its completion pinnacle by 1948 and '49 with the water system in place, the two lakes—dams. The second of the two was the primary water source and was stocked with fish. The Center boasted a filter plant, a reservoir, an electric pump which pumped water to a concrete storage tank. From there, it was piped to 20, modest buildings some clothed with an attractive skin of native rock and clay.

The terraced land allowed soil conservation. Over 140 acres were cultivated with approximately 1,600 fruit trees, most were peach with some fig and pecan trees. Texans came in droves to purchase what some said were the most delicious peaches in the state. (10) Three horses grazed meadows and fields, beside about 25 cows, and a large herd of goats which provided milk for Carmel's residents. Over 200 hens and a large apiary provided eggs and honey.

The dispensary not only administered first aid or minor treatments, it also housed a home for the aged. Davidians were noted for taking care of their infirm and elderly.

The printshop was the organization's life-blood, churning out literature by the millions for world-wide distribution. Presses often ran day and night.

In an article published July 10, 1948, the unique physical attributes of Mt. Carmel Center were summarized by Thomas Turner, from the "Central Texas Bureau of the News."

"A secluded little self-sustaining community that clings to a rocky ledge overlooking Lake Waco is the nerve center for a religious sect with a half million members scattered throughout the world.

"A sign at the gate-"Mount Carmel" is the only visible evidence to outsiders of the unique town within a city. The glare of publicity is not welcome at Mount Carmel.

"Very few people in Waco have any conception of the vast amount of work that goes on in the colorful native-stone buildings tucked away in the center of the dense timber.

"Mount Carmel is the world headquarters for a division of the Seventh-day Adventists.

"The Davidian division was founded by a short, sharp-eyed man named Brother Victor Houteff. Brother Houteff was born in Bulgaria, but he says he has forgotten how many years ago. The reason he has forgotten is that he doesn't believe in birthdays.

" 'I am still young because I never watch my age and mark off the years with birthdays,' explains Houteff.

"He looked about forty. He believes people would live ten years longer if they would adopt his system and forget birthdays.

"...With the aid of a dozen followers, he bought 180 wooded acres atop a bluff overlooking Lake Waco. Large portion of the land was on a rocky promontory which was considered worthless by the nearby landowners.

"Today the steep hill covered with elaborate terraces resembling the terraces that cling to Chinese and Japanese hillsides. Roads have been built throughout the settlement, which now totals 375 acres.

"Mount Carmel is ringed with evergreen bushes. It has two fine lakes formed by dams, and another on its way. It has its own water system.

"The most striking part of the settlement to the visitor who is lucky enough to get that far is the cluster of buildings that form the headquarters group.

"Built by the Adventists, the two largest buildings are made of white stones with red mortar. The red roofs are six inches thick, with rolling up and down contours.

"Altogether there are about twenty buildings, including living quarters, a cafeteria, hospital, chapel, garage and residences. One of the larger buildings contains a completely equipped store.

"The presses that print the bales of literature sent throughout the globe are in an air-conditioned building, which also houses the administrative offices.

"There are twenty-five acres of orchards and sixty-seven bee colonies. Much of its land is in cultivation, and the community has a big herd of dairy cattle.

"Ninety persons of all ages and from all sections of the United States work at Mount Carmel. They are carefully chosen by Houteff. They build new buildings and run the lumber yard, the laundry, and repair shops.

"Money is another subject Houteff does not like.

" 'No one is here for money motives,' " he says in his heavy accent. " 'Any profit that is shown at the end of the year goes back into Mount Carmel. We never worry about it.'

"Dollars, like birthdays, should not be counted too closely, he thinks."

This does not mean money was squandered. Association members were not wealthy. The majority were lower middle-class, or poor; thus the Association's income was quite limited. Its meager funds were used frugally. Otherwise, it could not have done so much, in such a short time, in the midst of the 1930's great depression. Mt. Carmel even had its own script which could be exchanged for standard currency from its Bank of Palestina.

The Davidic-Levitical Institute and Mt. Carmel Academy, its two educational subsidiaries, were also prominent features of Carmel's operations. The former, its ministerial school, was established in 1935 shortly after the Center's founding. Here young men acquired in-depth knowledge of the Bible—theology; the mechanics of presentation—homiletics, prophetic eschatology, biblical philosophy, sociology, history, and other Bible related academics.

Vocational training constituted part of the curriculum. (19) Students attended academic classes in the morning and worked in one of the Institution's departments in the afternoon. They pursued carpentry, mechanics, farming, or culinary arts. Efficient application, concentration, thoroughness, and speedy proficiency was stressed. Students not only learned to preach or teach but also to support themselves by their own labor. By these pursuits, they built character, strengthened independence, and self reliance, aided the Institution, and paid their own tuition. Though the curriculum was tough, students and staff adapted to and spoke highly of this method of education. Former Mt. Carmel residents, still remark on lessons learned in productivity and skills gained from Carmel's training. (10)

Of course, the Institute was not accredited and was not recognized by standard colleges. Accreditation was neither sought nor desired. The same held true for its academy. The obvious difference being the level and focus of study—general education or ministerial preparation. Education, in general, was key to the Center's work and the core of its purpose. In 1939, Houteff wrote, "Hence, for this more than for any other purpose, Mt. Carmel has been established. This education is, beyond a doubt, the greatest need of today." He also wrote, that this was the "...primary object of Mt. Carmel's existence..." (20)

He envisioned men and women becoming productive citizens, faithful examples to the efficacies of true Christianity. He believed that a well balanced education was a powerful testimony to Bible principles and would propel a nation to greatness.

Carmel's schools struggled to build students' character and personality, instilling usefulness. Houteff believed that much of mankind were spongers, non-producers. He believed that, in most cases, popular education encouraged selfishness; stifled individual reasoning from cause to effect. In 1939, he wrote this about education:

"The trouble is not with education itself, but rather with the kind of education one receives. Yes, there are two kinds of education—the human and the spiritual, the wrong and the right....It is recognized that the former is calculated to train the student, not to produce, but to consume—to be grasping and selfish; whereas the latter is designed to train the student to produce more than he consumes—to be benevolent and unselfish, living for others, not for self.

"...then, too, it must be realized that even if the schools were giving the right kind of training, it would be counteracted by parents who allow their children to squander away time, rather than teach them how to lighten someone's burdens and to make a living. So, if there is not mutual cooperation between the school and the home, then despite even a right educational system in the schools, the children would nevertheless be trained to become a burden to themselves, a liability to their parents, and a detriment to the world.

"...Necessarily, to make a real success in life, one must acquire a predominance of skills, superiority in a few, and distinct superiority in one; also a longing desire to please and bless others first, and only secondarily to satisfy himself....In such a happy course they will be benefiting themselves even more than others." (21)

It is now obvious why Mt. Carmel's schools did not seek accreditation. Although math, English, the sciences, history, social studies, and other common subjects were taught, the Bible played the major role. (2) Even those who later left the movement commended the Institution for an education that prepared them to bear life's burdens successfully. (10)

Delayed by the Center's arduous building schedule, the first ministerial students did not graduate until July 5, 1948. (22) Over the years, the Center sent many teachers throughout the Adventist world.

The academy was less successful. In 1948, it succumbed to a lack of financial support from parents. (20) Since many could not afford a private education, Mt. Carmel shouldered the lion's share of expenses. Parents in need paid only ten dollars a month. This 1940's bargain was granted to members who financially supported the Association regularly. This, coupled with rigidity in the school's program, contributed to the academy's closing, disappointing many, none more than Houteff. He felt that parents expected the school to train their children while they lent meager moral support.

Overall growth of the Association was unhindered. Tens of thousands of SDAs (concentrated largely in the Americas) were reached. By all appearances, Davidian SDAs were well on their way to touching every church member with their message. The Association did not intend to compete with secular or denominational institutions. Instead, it proclaimed a reformation that would reach over 800,000 Seventh-day Adventists. Davidians expected 144,000 (the group mentioned in Revelation—the Bible's last book) to embody their doctrines in principle and lifestyle. This 144,000 would complete the last phase of God's work—evangelizing the world. While not all, prophetically millions would accept the gospel invitation. They would establish the long awaited kingdom of eternal peace, a perfect society amidst a podigal generation— a testimony to God's love for mankind, his justice, and truth.

Mt. Carmel Center was thought to be the first step toward this grand scheme. Davidians believed that it could fully prepare the way for God's sealing of the 144,000 and subsequent establishment of the kingdom of unsurpassed glory. By the 1940s, the movement appeared well on its way to realizing this astounding goal.

Chapter 6

Inside Mt. Carmel Center

The most extraordinary feature of Mt. Carmel Center was its character—its peculiar, remarkable personality. Its uniqueness lay in its message, its mode and nature—not in its size, wealth, or ostentation.

Cultic groups existed then as they exist now with one dominating, central figure in control. Their constituencies, placed in abnormal mind-sets, separate themselves from their families, friends, and necessary non-religious activities. The outside world was often viewed as an enemy. Natural affections, and assets were redirected to that central person who often lived above rules and standards set for the group, including sexual exploitation. This was not the case with Mt. Carmel Center. On the contrary, outsiders may have accused them of Puritanism or Christian conservatism.

Teachings of moral rectitude guided adherents around life's precipitous curves. Houteff, who brought this advanced knowledge, was himself subject to its restrictions—subjected to the very same standards he himself taught; he was not the standard. Believers held that he was only the mouthpiece. He was the faucet, not the water, the eyes, not the view.

Many movements, in their beginnings, could make this idealistic summary. Their goals and objectives appeared noble and meritorious but soon became skewed and dangerously misguided. With the Davidian movement, this was not the case. Yes, they encountered dangers but not from cultic behavior; that would develop later from runaway groups.

Their message was the movement's engine; their faith its fuel; their efforts its wheels. Examining the spirit of Mt. Carmel Center, we can then understand Houteff and those who labored with him. Although, the secular world would have termed it quixotic fancy.

The lifestyle of Mt. Carmel's residents was strict. No one was forced or trapped into adopting it. All were vegetarians. Most were lacto-ovo vegetarians, consuming milk and eggs but no flesh foods whatsoever. They abstained from tabacco and alcohol. (1) This was mandatory and the recommended diet for all SDAs. Although not everyone followed this regimen, DSDAs did. Short skirts, short dresses, short sleeves were considered immodest. Low necklines, obviously tight-fitting clothing, certain types of makeup, rings, necklaces, and other jewelry were unacceptable. On the other hand slovenly attire was not appropriate either. Simplicity, quality, practicality was the standard. (2) Now, if you are thinking early 1800s, it was not like that either. Their dress code was on more modern lines, but modest—conservative. Yet, they were not conspicuous gazing stocks.

Residents were encouraged to attend devotional services each morning and evening. They had Sabbath (Saturday) afternoon worship after attending regular church services at local Seventh-day Adventist (SDA) churches.

Reverence was firmly upheld. Common whispering, laughing, talking, and unnecessary moving about before, during, or after meetings was considered offensive to God. (3) This reverence rule was so practiced that if a visitor whispered during a service, it would have been noticeably embarrassing.

Hard work was considered a productive character builder; a tool which made church members responsible, valuable assets to society. Even children worked, odd jobs, did chores, or assisted adults in their rounds. Less time spent in idle play, made them "producers" instead of "consumers." (4)

Many members had left jobs, education plans, numerous pursuits to man the Center. They hoped to usher in God's kingdom which they believed was very near. The Center regulated and disseminated this pulse of information. Rules and guidelines were strict to prepare a people for end-time events.

Besides dress and dietary guidelines, tight rules governed unguarded interaction between unmarried persons, cleanliness, loitering, complaints, and animal care. Gambling, profane language, obscene or questionable literature was prohibited. Gossip was frowned upon. (5) Although at times a challenging feat to accomplish, a spirit of unity and love was always encouraged.

The majority were white, but the 1940s and 50s brought more minorities to Mt. Carmel. Inspite of the Center's southern location, there was no record of racial incidents among "Rod" believers. Of course, this did not preclude prejudice within the local populace. Houteff once wrote in response to rumored racial discrimination:

"There are nearly four hundred acres of land on this hill, and we believe that we can serve all God's people regardless of color or race...for there should be no racial prejudice among God's people who are thoroughly converted." (6)

While racial flareups were not a concern on the hill, fire was. Wood stoves, kerosene lamps, open flame devices posed a disastrous threat. Wagon wheel bands with hammers hung as fire alarm systems. At the first sign of fire, residents hammered the band. Its loud clanging aroused the camp's bucket brigade.

During Carmel's existence, several insignificant fires did occur on rare occasion. One account gives a glimpse of life on Carmel's campus.

Before dawn on an ordinary, 1942 day, the dairyman hastened on his daily rounds. First he must start the kitchen's huge wood stove, then milk the cows and goats. He could hear them lowing for relief of their milky burdens. Unfortunately, he left a dish towel too close to the stove. (7)

Clang! Clang! Clanging jarred the early morning silence. Shouts of, "Fire! Fire!," tore the cool morning air. An unusual light glowed in the distance.

Like bees swarming a hive, residents grabbed buckets. Their brigade appeared as nothing against the unquenchable inferno. What more could they do? Consternation and dismay etched their faces in the eerie light. They stood to lose the kitchen and everything in it. They battled the blaze to no avail.

Then a familiar voice rang out over the confusion. "Put down your buckets." It was Houteff's distinct Bulgarian brogue. "Put down your buckets!...Only God can put out this fire!" He said in solemn demeanor. Hoping to rescue two important appliances, a Hobart and refrigerator, he continued, "Let us kneel down and ask the Lord to save what is left of our kitchen." (7)

With sweaty brows and the kitchen an uncontrollable blaze, they knelt as Houteff prayed a simple prayer. Opening their eyes, they were delighted to find the fire completely out. Appliances and what was left of the kitchen, saved. (7)

April 6, 1943 brought another crisis. The second dam, "Lake Meribah," with earthen walls over 40' high, about 2 1/2-3 miles in circumference, threatened to give way. The Conservation Core was called in to avert certain disaster for residents on Highway 6. If Lake Meribah Dam collapsed, it meant unprecedented catastrophe for Waco.

They discovered that because of a construction error the dam had no spillway to alleviate existing pressure. After gauging the situation, The Conservation Core declared the job too dangerous. They refused to try mending the dam, because that could cause the break even sooner. In their situation assessment, evacuation was the answer. Procedures were quickly implemented.

It was up to the Davidians to do something. But what? Mending the dam seemed suicidal. Yet they could not allow the dam to break, destroying lives and property. Negative publicity could severely mar their work and ruin Davidia's reputation.

In a show of appreciation to the Core for coming, Davidians fed them and made them comfortable. Then Houteff summoned the head of each family to pray for the dam. Afterward, he instructed them to make a spillway, using sandbags, shovels, and bulldozers. "You'll be safe...," Houteff insisted. "It won't break." He was certain God would preserve them from all harm. They went to work. The dam held without loss of life or property. The Conservation Core, local residents, and Mt. Carmel Center residents witnessed an unforgettable example of faith in action. (7)

No question about it, these Adventists were committed. During the Center's development, from 1930 to 1943, members were earnest. Lacking money or college degrees, believers may have appeared as unlikely choices for God's representatives. They may have appeared as rough, uninviting, unrefined misfits. Their mere existence challenged SDA church hierarchy. Their unpleasing message called the church to reform, and announced God's judgment imminent because of the denomination's backsliding. They sounded the alarm of biblical prophets who had warned ancient Israel of God's impending wrath, pleading in dour but poetic, tender terms. "The Shepherd's Rod" was seen as a modern alarm calling present-day Israel, the SDA denomination, to reform and return to the God who loved them.

Believers felt that one character in the Bible aptly fit them, David. From him they drew their name, "Davidian." While still a lad, David slew the giant Goliath when all others cowed at the colossal challenge. (8) It was to David, the illustrious king of Jewish antiquity, that the eternal kingdom had been promised. Furthermore, in some places in the Old Testament the church was termed "The House of David."

Though not generally adopted until 1942, the title "Davidian" was used to avoid accusations of misrepresentation. (9, 10) Previously, Adventists who embraced the "Rod's" message were called "Shepherd's Rod Seventh-day Adventists." (11) In fact, the official name of the Association after moving to Waco in 1935, was "The General Association of The Shepherd's Rod Seventh-day Adventists." (10, 11)

The Association was not recognized by the US government as an ecclesiastical body. It did not have formal membership nor claim to be distinct and separate from the Seventh-day Adventist denomination. Believers did not desire formal registration and did not endeavor to establish a separate world church. Unforeseen circumstances, however, dictated the need for formal registration.

When the US entered World War II, the Association's men faced the Draft as conscientious objectors thus needing proof of church membership. (12) SDA denominational leaders denied all students of Houteff's message this right. The Association was forced to adopt a constitution, create by-laws, and register as an organization. At that time, the name "Davidian" was used and published in a booklet entitled "The Leviticus of Davidian Seventh-day Adventists," outlining its constitution, by-laws, origin, and aims.

Houteff wrote in 1942, "Having now, though, at the closing of its twelfth year progressed to the publication of the 'Leviticus,' the Association receives from this governmental organ, the name, Davidian Seventh-day Adventists. No longer, therefore does it borrow its name from its publications. (10)

The Association issued membership certificates. "Because a number of Davidian Seventh-day Adventists have been confronted with the need of identifying their church membership, and because the mother Seventh-day Adventist denomination denies this privilege to them, the Davidian Seventh-day Adventists Association has prepared a membership certificate for all who are eligible and who desire to have one." (12) The Association was registered, but was not designated as a separate world church. It was and is a religious association operating independent of the General Conference of SDA's, yet generically "within the Seventh-day Adventist organization." (13)

The preface of its constitution states, "Provisional in its setup as well as in name, the Davidian Seventh-day Adventists Association exists soley to accomplish a divinely appointed work within the Seventh-day Adventist denomination, wherein it therefore strictly confines its activities." (13)

Up to Houteff's death in 1955, the Association's activities were strictly confined to Adventists in compliance with its charter. Workers and ministers traveled throughout the US, Canada, the Caribbean, and parts of Central and South America, but largely kept their work within Adventism.

True Davidians neither build their own houses of worship, nor hold their own church services. Instead, they worship with their Adventist counterparts in local SDA churches, to the dismay of church leaders. Doing otherwise is considered a grave violation of their message.

Attending local church services often brought conflict and persecution to Davidians. Sometimes, they were physically assaulted or verbally bashed, usually without provocation. Just the presence of a

Davidian could spark indignities from conference leadership.

Most Davidians were members of local churches or were conference workers who had made some contribution to the world church, but they were quickly excommunicated after embracing the "Rod's" message. Davidians' efforts to call forth a reformation within the denomination were unappreciated. Wild, strange stories circulated about Davidians. These stories formed mountains of prejudice and ostracism in the SDA mind. Yet, Davidians refused to form their own denomination. As a result, they were viewed as a plague, Adventism's perpetual annoyance. Some of these stories still circulate today, creating misapprehension and insurmountable prejudice.

Davidians supported the Association with at least a tenth of their earnings (tithe). Some gave two tithes. They remitted offerings to their local SDA conference congregation to assist operating expenses. Houteff, himself, encouraged this practice (although not necessarily during church services). (7)

The work's difficulty forced them to seek creative means to reach church members. Davidians acquired names and addresses from those bold enough to give them and sent lists to Mt. Carmel Center. In turn, literature was sent to SDA homes. Some believers held discussions immediately after church services, or on Sabbath afternoons in homes of the curious or genuinely interested. Perhaps this method was the most successful. During such discussions, people studied with more objectivity, listened to a more detailed presentation, allowing understanding of the Davidian perspective. The vast majority, however, were too fearful to investigate. Consequently, they knew little or nothing of the truth concerning Davidians and their message. After Houteff's death, literature was sometimes given en masse at Adventist gatherings. (7)

A large percentage of those who spent time understanding the message became believers, or were more sympathetic toward the movement. When several church members accepted the new teachings they would organize a company or group in their locality. The Association coordinated and supported these companies. They sent supplies of literature, Davidian ministers, or Bible workers, and funds when necessary. Many of these companies, scattered throughout the world, met after regular church services on Saturday afternoons. In some instances, whole congregations embraced the new light. A precise record of the number of companies organized does not exist. However, tiny rivulets of believers formed a cascade of the Davidian movement. A believer here, a believer there, A company here, a company there, all contributed to the growing expanse. The field, as they called it, was the network of the Association. Mt. Carmel Center was the hub of an expansive wheel of truth seekers.

With the organizational flavor of a corporation, it had an executive council and assorted departments or divisions. (14) In 1943, salaried ministerial staff totaled 22. Bible workers numbered 35. These figures excluded department heads and regular staff. Obviously, it would not rank with the Fortune 500 corporations of today, but it was one of the largest operations of its kind. Well organized, it reached hundreds of thousands worldwide.

Advances were not made without sacrifice. funds were low, helpers few. Staffers often held multiple positions. Operating on a financial "shoestring," workers garnered a subsistence wage. In 1938, the institution could finally afford paying its workers. They received 14 cents an hour. The 1940's saw an increase in salaries. Bonuses were given for outstanding work or expertise in a particular skill. The prevailing wisdom was that "some lines of work should pay more than others." Student staffers were paid 3 1/2 to 13 cents an hour, depending on the quality of their work and type of skills. (15)

The Association took good care of all residents, and required that able bodies work in whatever capacity they could. No one lived at another's expense. No one individual lived wealthy while others struggled to subsist. No matter one's background, station, or education, all were classed as colleagues. All were expected to give and work according to their abilities.

After appropriate remittances, funds recycled into the Association. Not even Houteff, president and prophet, held a higher material status. He did not own a home. He paid many workers more than he paid himself. (16) He owned an old Ford. He did not personally benefit from the organization—perhaps to circumvent any misconception of his earnest commitment to the cause.

Wearing his favorite sweater and run-over shoes, his unassuming demeanor disarmed the suspicious. On the other hand, his attire was not untidy, unkept, or offensive. While conducting business off campus or shopping in town, he wore suits. (7)

Houteff was neither boisterous nor eccentric or reclusive. He was cheerful and often playful with children. He had an uproarious laugh. Yet, he was not prankish or petty. Those who knew him well saw that he loved people, but he was somewhat reserved. One Bible worker remembered returning from missionary service, and meeting Houteff for the first time. He was received with an unhesitated, affectionate embrace. (7)

Not a talkative man, yet, when he spoke his words evoked thought. His admonitions, warnings, or suggestions sooner or later proved true. By most followers he was viewed as the last of the prophets before the coming of God's kingdom. His messages, written or verbal, were considered as inspired as SDA's considered Mrs. White's messages inspired. However, their inspiration came in different ways.

Mrs. White often had visions, dreams, or was believed to have been guided by an angel or heavenly agent who assisted her in understanding Scripture, individual lives, or circumstances.

Mr. Houteff never reported having visions or special dreams. Yet, he presented some of the most convincing expositions of passages of Scripture that, up to his time, were considered mysteries. Reportedly a calm, still voice directed him. (7)

He never bluntly claimed prophetic status. Neither did Mrs. White. Neither did they disclaim the title nor rebuffed anyone who called them such. They made it plain; their instructions were to be taken as if coming from God. Doing otherwise, after clearly understanding their messages, imperiled one's soul. On the other hand, they did not claim infallibility or that their writings superseded the Bible. (17, 18, 19) On the contrary, they insisted, their messages led to and were in perfect harmony with the Bible. (20)

They believed they were Scripture's magnifiers—inspired teachers to be tested and proved by the Bible. They were not extra-biblical sources nor the only mediums through whom God worked. All such claimants must pass Scriptures' testing. These issues on inspiration are extremely important areas when trying to understand Adventism, the Davidian movement and associated events. We will explore this further.

Houteff was questioned that if he was a prophet from God, why did he not have trance visions? His answer: "Supernatural experiences are not the strongest evidence of one's connection with Divine power. In fact, they are not necessarily proof at all, for there are many doctrines and faith built upon one miracle or another, and yet devoid of truth. Neither should one forget that not all the prophets of the Bible had trance visions. David and Solomon recorded, not what was given them in vision, but what they received through other means. John the Baptist was called even more than a prophet, yet there is not a single prophetic utterance recorded by him, nor is there any record that he was ever taken into trance and given visions. He was merely an interpreter of the writings of the prophets." (21)

Houteff's calling was said to be that of an interpreter of the Scriptures. Like William Miller, founder of early Adventism, he believed the Bible explained itself. An interpretive prophet provided the key to unlock its many mysteries. Books like "Revelation," "Daniel," "Ezekiel," became easier to understand once the messenger, under divine enlightenment, broke the divine code.

Time and space preclude delving into details of his views on the role of a modern-day Bible prophet. However, the following may be helpful in conveying the concept.

"Now with all respect and sincerity, by the authority of the Scriptures and by virtue of the facts before me, I say that it would be easier for a chicken to find its roost in the blackest of night than for uninspired minds to unveil the prophecies and the parables. The difference between the two is that the chicken realizes the futility of trying to find her roost after sunset, but the self-willed man does not realize that he cannot unveil Truth at his own will and without light from above.

"We as Christians have obviously failed to note that if the secret things of God, matter not how simple, were to be unsealed at any time by anyone, Inspiration [God] would never in the first place have concealed them in symbols and parables. Christendom is still blind to the fact that to attempt to break into these mysteries of God would be to attempt to defeat His purposes; yes, to try to break into the Divine code, is to try the impossible...Then how can we do such before time?" (22) Brackets ours.

Houteff was convinced the time had come for God to reveal the mysteries of "Revelation" and other baffling Scriptures. Hence the need of modern-day, inspired messengers—prophets—to whom God could grant those mysteries' key.

How would one recognize a genuine prophet? The person's character and life would harmonize with righteous principles. White and Houteff agreed that a true messenger would lead to perfect harmony with the Bible. A true prophet would allow Scriptures to explain themselves with clarity. A true prophet would not force or twist their meanings out of context to fit cherished views.

The Bible is somewhat like a jigsaw puzzle. Each piece must fit its assigned position to obtain a proper picture. A new message should lead the message bearer to greater heights of integrity based on biblical principles. Anything less brands the purported messenger as an imposter.

Houteff wrote of events past and present which were unthinkable in his time. In the 1940's, he wrote of movements toward a "new world order"—an upcoming union of nations under the United Nations; the establishment of the state of Israel; the present raging battle between labor and management; and the ecumenical movement. He wrote of, what he termed, the "greatest of all battles," a war in the Middle East. He foretold winners and losers of this battle we may term World War III. He predicted the apparent fall of Communism and union of churches; and even the breakup of the Davidian movement. His pen chronicled science, education, nutrition, psychology, and of course, theology.

Davidians saw him as God's messenger. His sermons, his

counsels, his concepts and insights (not his everyday speech) were labeled inspired. He had final say on all pertinent matters.

Houteff was respected as a prophet. Yet, there is no real evidence that he ever acted the role of an autocrat or despot. He was emphatic on a particular view only when he felt strongly it was from God. In those cases, even the executive council yielded to his judgment.

He could not have contradicted biblical basics, or already established doctrines. For example, he could not have chosen two wives or declared himself God in the flesh. He could not have changed his choice of the day of worship from Sabbath (Saturday) to Sunday. He would have been quickly denounced, by Adventists, as a false teacher. He, too, must work within bounds of the principles and dogmas he presented as truth. There was no room for cultic behavior.

The Davidian movement was not based on a singular figure. Davidians believed that they followed a power greater than Houteff, greater than any man, no matter how honored. Unfortunately, many would later lose sight of this. So, Houteff was not to enjoy a ministry of all freedom.

Fanaticism became a perilous foe to Davidia after Houteff's death. Even while he lived, its venom seeped in but was held in check. As the Association grew, some clung to the theology but departed from early simplicity, self-denial, and pioneer goals. It appeared that they did not understand the message or the work. They had one agenda the Association had another. They seemed to have had a blurred focus and imbalanced religious perceptions. Some twisted or strained one doctrine or another out of proportion which gave birth to outlandish teachings.

On the other side of the spectrum, a vast majority clung to Houteff as if he were an icon—fanaticism or flattery. It was hard to tell which class irritated him the most. The former he disdained in all guises. He gave extremism no chance to flourish. As for the latter, he never sought praise, he instead rebuked it.

While Houteff lived the movement prospered. However, his ministry was not opposition free. He fought fanaticism, conquered constant murmuring and complaining. After his death, bad decisions caused fragmentation, disappointment, and the eventual closing of Mt. Carmel Center, causing splinter groups. Beside the denomination's persecution and extremism in Davidia, he faced the church's attack in other areas. SDA denominational leaders had accused him of concentrating administrative power in his family's hands. (23) It was true that most of the Executive Council officers were his family members. He was president; his wife, Florence, was secretary. Sopha Hermanson, his mother-in-law, was treasurer. The one exception, vice president, E.T. Wilson, a former SDA conference president. There is no record of Houteff's family abusing their positions or personally benefiting from their power.

Davidians may argue that administration by family group is not an uncommon, unbiblical occurrence. Moses, Israel's great emancipator, was its chief executive officer. His brother, Aaron occupied the second highest post in the nation as high priest. His sister, Miriam, was prophetess and music leader. According to Old Testament Scripture, God Himself appointed them. (24, 25, 26)

Mrs. E.G. White was considered a prophetess in SDA circles, Her husband, James, served as an SDA General Conference president for years. In other words, it amounted to trust. Houteff chose persons whom he believed would not abuse their trust.

The Executive Council's organization changed in 1948. A council was installed that did not include previous positions, but it still reported to the primary officers.

Houteff's personal life was also attacked. His marriage was questioned on two counts by the denomination, and some Davidians. First, it was alleged that he had two wives. Second, he was considered a cradle robber for marrying Florence. At the time of their marriage, in 1937, he was about 52; she was 19 or 20. Realizing the damage these rumors could cause, Houteff responded in an article.

"Satan never tells the truth; thus he has used his agents to spread many false reports such as the foregoing ones concerning Brother Houteff; who was a single man when eighteen years ago, he came in contact with the Seventh-day Adventist message, and who at no time during these years has divorced anyone, or married any-one save the one with whom he now lives." (27)

Regarding age, he cited Abraham who married his second wife, Keturah, who was still of child bearing years and Abraham was about 140. Houteff cited Isaac, Boaz, Esther as further examples. (27) He continued his pointed rebuttal.

"The trouble is not with Brother Houteff's marriage, but rather with those who judge Brother Houteff by their own standards. Had Brother Houteff married for the same reason that most others marry, then, of of course, he could have taken a wife of almost any age, and it would have made no great difference to him. But Brother Houteff's critics seem utterly to forget that he has a tremendous work, and that he does not need a wife able only to make a home for him, but rather one most able to assist him in his work. Hence, and aged woman, or one without experience in the work would be to him a hindrance rather than a help."(27)

Florence Hermanson, daughter of Sophe Hermanson, grand daughter of Mrs. Charboneau (the first to fully embrace the "Rod") was a highly respected, committed Davidian. Young Florence was mature for her age. She was exemplary in conduct and demeanor, talented, working diligently to promote the cause. (7) The family's extraordinary commitment and Florence's faith in the message, played a primary part in Houteff's uniting his life with hers.

Accounts depict her as the quintessential Christian woman, capable, but never boastful or proud. (7) She was taller than her husband. Her slender frame accented her sharp cheeks and gentle smile and was always complemented by modest apparel.

Unfortunately, after Victor Houteff's death, circumstances weighed her with decisions that changed her life, the Center's destiny, and Davidia's history forever. Those few years were perhaps the most trying of her life. They etched her memory with pictures of a time and place she could never erase no matter how hard she tried.

Although he seemed to love children, they had none. As to why? We do not have a clue. Some speculated, having a modern-day prophet for a father would have placed children in a precarious position. Others suspected, having children would have hampered the Houteff's extremely demanding work for the Association.

These matters, however, were not to be the most hazardous to the movement. Fanaticism and idolization of Houteff were the most venomous. We view this in several accounts.

We do not know the exact year. We do know it was a Sabbath afternoon in the 1940's. Houteff's customary sermon that day was on a text from Joel. Houteff was an interesting speaker but not prone to showing emotions. However, on that day, he seemed overwhelmed or enraptured with the sense of the text. As he neared the end of his discourse, tears streamed down his cheeks. He cried out, "It's worth it folks!...It's worth it!" (7)

Also clutched by emotion, one member poured accolades, praising Houteff for the light he had brought them. Another chimed in. Suddenly, the voice from the pulpit blared, "Don't you ever...ever give me credit for this truth." The congregation hushed, shocked by his uncharacteristic pungent rebuff. No doubt, the members praising him meant well, but Houteff knew it must be stopped. Condoning such action would strengthen the growing tendency to place too much confidence in him. He was the messenger, not the source of the message. He desired for them to look to a higher spring of knowledge.

His response did not completely stop the undercurrent of man-worship. Years later, many promoted the idea that Houteff would never die. Sickened by such nonsense, he publicly denounced the concept. (7)

In 1951, John Kelly, a member in his 30's, came to Mt. Carmel Center. Why he came was unclear. Possibly, he came to work in the rest home. It did not take long before he questioned and quibbled the diet of Mt. Carmel residents. He scolded staff members and complained about the Institution's "sinful" use of diary products.

In the dining room one day, Kelly began his regular harangue against using milk and eggs. Houteff, possibly prompted by Kelly's macerated appearance, asked, "How much work have you done today, Bro. Kelly?"

"I cannot work, because I'm sick." Kelly replied.

Houteff retorted, "These people have worked 8-10 hours a day and they are getting along with this diet just fine. What's wrong with your health reform? It sounds like health deform!...If you would drink a little bit of milk, Brother Kelly, I'd think you would feel a lot better and feel stronger."

Strange as it may sound, the account tells us that, the next morning found Kelly lapping milk from a bowl like a dog. Houteff saw this strange behavior. Placing his arms around Kelly, in pitying tones he said, "I'm sorry, Brother Kelly. I did not realize...I did not know...Come with me." Kelly was later taken to a mental facility in Austin, Texas. (7)

Bachand, another member, claimed his pregnant wife would give birth to the biblical Baby Jesus. (7)

Unfortunately, there were some who sympathized with this outlandish theory. After some time, hoping the vain thing would die of itself, hoping those believing the fantasy would recognize their folly, Houteff called a residents' meeting. He pleaded and reasoned from logic and Scripture.

"It's beyond me how anyone could accept this foolishness." Houteff said, bewildered. "What's in your mind?..."

Bachand was adamant. He would not relinquish his idea, but determined to push it. Houteff could not allow the situation to continue. Protecting the Association's work from disreputable fallout, Bachand was kindly asked to leave Mt. Carmel Center.

Houteff's pointedness was one of his outstanding characteristics. Never rude or uncouth, he was plainspoken. He dealt boldly with matters of special importance, disturbing circumstances, inequities, deceptions, cruelties, fanaticism. Extremism in health issues was one matter that lured his frankness.

He was a strong advocate of preventive or alternative medicine. But he was ridiculed for condoning use of prescription drugs under certain circumstances by those who decried drug use under any circumstances. Finally, in a letter dated October 12, 1952, Houteff reprimanded the no-druggers.

"If these fanatical no-druggers had remedies to replace drugs in the treatment of critically acute and deadly diseases...then there would be justification in their indiscriminately condemning drugs. As it is now, though, their condemnation of all drugs for all people under all circumstances, and at the same time their utter failure to save the victims in all such cases from either death or excruciating suffering, is folly and madness...

"They may contend that prayer will do all this. But if these misguided enthusiasts are sure of the efficacy of their prayers, why are they not operating wonder working, crowd-packed prayer clinics for the alleviation and elimination of human suffering, thus discrediting and outmoding modern medical science? Why leave millions to suffer along in the hands of the medical profession if they have something better for them!

"We certainly know that prayer has been efficacious in many cases; but aside from counterfeits, we know of no healers [no-druggers] doing business wholesale fashion...

"Some months back I had to deal with fanatics right here at Mt. Carmel. In order to satisfy them and myself as well as those who were sympathetic with them, I gave them what they wanted: part of our hospital building and whatever equipment and supplies they had to have, then bid them God's speed. But what happened? Nothing more than to splatter around for about two months, then they suddenly vacated and left everybody in disgust...

"Now if they feel better and want to try it again we will give them another opportunity...We are determined to do right, obey the Truth, and to be taught any good thing by anyone. This is the best we can do and it's the best we can be expected to do...

"The modern drugless cult, however, either ignorant of the subject, or zeal-filled for a following or for business, are disseminating their fanatical doctrines and causing confusion, unnecessary suffering and untimely deaths. Sister White had to contend with the same kind of trouble." (28)

Houteff also challenged folk who liberally criticized Mt. Carmel's management. The following excerpt is from a letter written to an unnamed believer. It was published in the May/June 1937,

"Symbolic Code," the Association's newsletter. It presented revealing passages regarding his personal frustrations in the work and marked clues to his personality.

"At any rate, as you think that some improvements must be made in the management, then why are you 'waiting for results'? Why not come to the help of the Lord? Truly, Brother_____, those who are best equipped to take any active part in the work, are the very ones who are waiting to see 'results' from us fellows who have neither talent nor experience....

"Pardon me, Brother_____, but I think you are mistaken in saying that Brother Houteff 'does not realize that he is attempting too great a problem in undertaking to manage everything,' for I am in a better position than anyone else to know whether or not I realize my problems. I am not by choice, but rather by necessity, undertaking to manage 'everything.' Those who could and should be helping in the management have left me to do the work with children, sick women, and crippled men, while those who might be helping me are standing afar off, criticizing and waiting for 'results.' Yes, I am undertaking more than you perhaps will ever know—more, because in part, even those who are competent physicians, have left also their work for me to do, and are themselves doing nothing to help us in our physical infirmities but to 'occupy...time...and wait results.'...

"Today I had to treat six patients, and my wife had to treat two more. I then went to town to purchase a tire for our truck, and helped put it on, after which I wrote five letters, besides this one; edited the entire Code manuscript; not mentioning other business problems that called for my attention all day long. Yes, I even had to go twice to the farm to look after things; once to the dam to take care of an injured horse; twice to the water tank project; and drew plans for the tank and for other building construction.

"While writing this, I was interrupted by a sudden call, and have just gotten through bandaging a certain brother's fractured chest. And as the clock is about to strike 9:30 p.m., I shall retire at this juncture to rest until the rising bell rings at 5:00 a.m..

"Good morning, Brother_____! Though I intended to

rest until 5:00 o'clock, I awakened early, finding my mind possessed of the same thoughts that were there when I went to sleep last night, and as my sleep was gone, I felt that I had better get to my duties for the day, by endeavoring to finish my writing to you. It is now 3:45 a.m.." (29)

It disappointed Houteff to see this criticizing, extreme element creep into the Association. He realized that fanaticism and disaffection hampered the work. Later, he summarized his feelings and the feelings of many of the followers.

"Though at times we are greatly disappointed as we see among us the unfaithful, fault-finding, self-exalting multitude...along with those who apparently believe and who declare that they stand strongly for the message, but who are throwing rocks at us and at our work; though we certainly are not grateful for this element yet we are not at all discouraged..." (30) In spite of some discordant elements, the Association continued to grow. Houteff continued to write and speak. It appeared that nothing would deter the Movement. Davidians were a permanent patch in the fabric of Adventism. Although tattered in places, they formed an unbroken pattern.

Chapter 7

Message Like None Other

The secular world may view the Davidian movement as an example of man's capacity for self-deception, his innate desire to satisfy his spiritual hunger. The religious world may mistake it for another group of misguided enthusiasts. Whatever one's opinion of Davidia, a conscientious study of their message will leave a lasting impression. Unbiased study may leave a lingering conviction of its veracity or repulse you, but it will affect you. Effects are more profound upon an Adventist who holds, in common with Davidians, the same fundamental beliefs.

Davidians, their work, their message, have been misunderstood, misquoted, and distorted. Some Davidians, themselves, have added to this unfortunate circumstance by monomania or one craze or another. We discussed this in the last chapter. However, when we refer to the Davidian message, we are referring to the original message Victor Houteff presented as the "The Shepherd's Rod."

Those who later launched their own message, borrowed themes from the Bible, Mrs. White's writings, and Houteff. They mixed in their own views and developed doctrines completely different from those of the original, a kind of doctrinal cakemaking. Retaining similar terms and names, they formed a quasi relationship. This blurred matters for unwary seekers who sometimes rejected the original "Rod," thinking they had studied it when they really had not.

The true Davidian message provided challenging theology. Some modern-day theologians may question the rules Davidians used to arrive at their unpopular interpretations and conclusions. This is undaunting since theologians and biblical experts disagree among themselves on methodology used to interpret numerous passages of Scripture. Actually, the whole matter can be down-right confusing. Houteff was certain that the Bible was God's word and that it alone held the true meaning of life and accurately presaged the future of mankind. Luminaries, great thinkers, great intellects, were just rills from the fountain of all knowledge—God. Although betrayed by its stewards, and embattled by its enemies, Houteff believd that true Judeo-Christian ideals will stand, outlasting Humanism and Socialism in all their forms. To be fair to him, it must also be pointed out that Houteff did not advocate the so-called "Victorian" era, or middle-age Christianity. True Christianity, he constantly pointed out, is "progressive." Unfortunately, enlightened Christianity is rarely witnessed and has become a contemptuous rag, a moral dwarf-explaining its inability to substantially impact western or eastern society.

His message predicted world events and circumstances years before their development or inception. In this chapter we will examine some of these projections, challenging those inclined to discount the "Rod" out of hand. Unfortunately, new ideas and concepts are not readily embraced. It may take years before they are even considered an option, or given proper reception or recognition. Religion, which should lead in objectivity, is unwittingly its worse enemy.

Before discussing the "Rod's" highlights, we must understand its cellular level. It is not important to delve into theology and its obscure language. However, it is essential to discuss briefly Houteff's method of interpretation. Why? The answer is simple. Understanding the route one took to a destination, makes all the difference in the world in accepting the nuances of arrival. Whether one enjoys the journey or is pleased with the destination is another matter.

Houteff took the position of his forerunners—leaders of the Protestant Reformation and those of the 1840's advent movement—that the Bible is Its own expositor. The Bible is not simply a book of narratives but a collage of truth revealed through history, poetry, prophecy, parables, and letters, precise as an architect's plan.

Although It was written by many authors, in some cases hundreds of years apart, careful study reveals Its perfect harmony with every part of Itself. The Bible must be understood as It reads unless figures or symbolical language is used. When facing the latter, a diligent search must be made throughout the Bible to determine that figure or symbol's meaning. If one can form an interpretation without contradicting other portions of Scripture pertaining to the subject at hand, it is a true interpretation. To know whether a historical event fulfilled prophecy, one must find every word of that prophecy literally met within the event. But if one word lacks proof of fulfillment, one must search further or await future development. Houteff put it this way:

"Affirmatively stated, all Scripture, not merely a part of it, is inspired. Negatively stated, none of it is privately interpreted, for the reason that it did not come of men but of God; that is as the Spirit of God dictated to men the Scriptures, so the Spirit of God must interpret the Scriptures to men..." (1)

This comment may spark fierce debate. To Davidians it is the only way to understand the Bible and avoid Christendom's mass confusion. "We should now be convinced," Houteff continued, "that as long as this Divine command and principle of interpreting God's Word is overlooked and abused, and as long as selfishness and bigotry exist among Christians in general and among Bible students in particular, isms will continue to increase, and the strength of the people will continue to be wasted..." (1)

Interestingly enough, Houteff forecasted numerous events and circumstances, but never once set dates. After his death, steps taken in that direction would sully the movement. Subsequent time-setting predictions marked the work of spurious leaders. Their actions brought near disaster to the movement and fuel to its opponents. These extremists ignored Mrs. White's counsel and Houteff's admonitions against time-setting. "The message ['The Shepherd's Rod'] sets no date, either exact or approximate..." (2) [] Brackets ours. A stand which he maintained until his death.

Although he did not set dates, his insight was far-reaching. For example, his comments on current events predicted a future one world-international federation of nations, known today as the "new world order." He also forecast major steps leading to this huge world order which began just before World War II. To acquire a fair grip of his views, we need to briefly encapsulate some key features.

Houteff foresaw the Second World War, the formation of the United Nations, the establishment of the State of Israel, and the rise of Communism as a super-power. This, to us, is all history but was prophetic to those living in the 1940's.

Houteff believed the Bible clearly predicted the fall of the western world (particularly the US), Israel, and Arabs in an unprecedented world war. It does not end there. He also believed the Bible revealed results of this mind boggling scenario. Under influence of a church or Christian Coalition, the US will throw out her constitution. Partnered with the remainder of the western world, she will establish a super-church-state system—a one world government uniting economics, politics, and religion—"The New World Order."

What about Communism? Houteff said interesting things about that, too. He did not envision Communism's death or a lasting end of the cold war. He perceived an immutable struggle between West and East until the "New World Order's" formation. Applying his teachings to today's situation, it means Communism is not dead and will come again to the forefront.

On September 30, 1939, and again on June 22, 1940, Houteff made the following statements during his Sabbath (Saturday) afternoon talk, expounding on the eighth chapter of Isaiah he said:

"God here is challenging a move toward a federation of nations. With World War I we began to hear serious proposals for the associating of nations into a single league. Today the proposal is revived, and efforts are being made toward forming a strong and workable union of nations. Indeed, not only is the idea of international federation growing more and more prevalent, but in the minds of many great men, there is the positive conviction that the successful continuance of their nation's way of life is utterly dependent upon the closest association and cooperation of all those nations which share their way of life....

"...There may be some significance in the repetition of the warning. If so, it would indicate that either two or possibly three attempts would be made among nations to associate and gird themselves..." (3)

These statements were first made at the outset of hostilities in Europe which led into the Second World War—before England fully

engaged in the war, before the Western Alliance and the United States' entrance into the war, before the formation of United Nations.
He did not say exactly when this international confederacy would take place, but he did give some clues. He went on to say, "...the confederacy is formed when the nations are girding themselves for war." (4)

In 1942, he gave two sermons on the same topic. He said, "After Isaiah mentions the ancient historical confederacy...verse 9 of chapter 8 warns against another association of peoples, saying that this confederacy will likewise surely fail and fall to pieces." (5)

Most Davidians scoured the news with profound interest to see if World War II would fulfill prophecy. Or would it be another signpost pointing to a greater war and international alliance. To them this war was pivotal to the biblical, prophetic record—representing crowning truth which would purify His church, leaving a group of outstanding Christians who would perfectly represent Him to a dying world. Christians who would usher in the eternal kingdom, and finish the gospel commission, taking it throughout the globe. Since Houteff had indicated that perhaps "two or possibly three attempts would be made," (3) they watched and waited.

During the war, Houteff wrote extensively on events expected to come to fruition. But he believed they would only see fulfillment if the church was ready. (6, 7) If not, some would be fulfilled and the remainder relegated to the future.

After the bombing of Pearl Harbor, the US entered the war—the world, by 1941, was engulfed in a gigantic war. The stage was set for the prophecies to unfold.

One event's expected fulfillment was the fall of western powers—primarily England, France, the United States, and their allies. Houteff believed the Bible clearly outlined this. Therefore, during the war, Davidians were somewhat diffident to its outcome. Would their hopes for the kingdom be realized, or must they continue their difficult labors? Were they standing at the open doors of God's glorious kingdom? Or were they approaching another passageway into more time, more hope, more faith. Houteff too awaited the outcome.

After the war, he made more astounding assertions. He bib-

lically explained what had happened and what was expected in the future. Summarily, he declared that
World War II was a prime indicator of an even greater war and greater alliance. His exact words were:

"Then, too, the defeat of Japan and of Germany has by no means ended the war. It has only deepened the international deadly wound.... As far as Inspiration is concerned, World War Two has not ended.

"This in itself is evidence enough that the world now, during this period of international unrest such as it has never before had—unrest that is caused by every existing element—is to give birth to something." (8)

"Moreover," he wrote again, "the fact that only verse 44 [of Daniel chapter eleven] so far has been fulfilled, that the king [the western world] is yet to come to his end, is proof positive that World War Two is yet to be finished, that there is to be no peace now, and no mutual agreement between the nations although the war is supposed to have ceased since Hitler's disappearance." (9) [] Brackets ours.

Concerning further attempts to establish global unification, in 1948 he wrote:

"Anyone can see that world is fast getting ready to resume the war with a mightier and final blow if possible. Anyone can see, too, that the war was not won for the good of Great Britain, but for Russia, and that following the cessation of hostilities conditions have caused the world to consolidate into two great and hostile blocks,—not to mention the wars and rumors of wars all around us...

"Let me remind you of what Inspiration has to say of the association of nations and peoples according to current events. For light on the subject we turn to the eighth chapter of Isaiah's prophecy... You remember that the chapter unveils a [ancient] confederacy... Inspiration makes a type of that church and state confederacy, and by it definitely points out the trend which the nominal churches and the sovereign powers of the world are to take now in the antitype. It makes known, moreover, that they will not prosper in it...

"From these scriptures it is seen that the current events brought about by the two opposing blocks, the east and the west, are not going to work out according to human planning, that the plans made by the confederation of nations and peoples are to come to naught..." (10)

These statements were made shortly after World War II, before the cold war between Communism and the West, before Russia became a world super-power. The end result of this cold war? Another World War! No one, not even the United Nations will be able to check this next conflagration.

Will conflagration III start in Europe? No, says Houteff. The Middle East! "Just how this is to come about," he said, "I do not know; but I do know that the greatest of all wars is to be fought about the holy land..." (10)

This war is a distinct and separate war from Armageddon referred to, for many years, by various Christian commentators. Houteff's Middle East war precedes the popular Armageddon which begins further down the prophetic line.

His predictions concerning results of this Middle East war is more surprising: "In that battle the nations will defeat the rulers of the Promised Land: (11) According to Houteff, today's Jerusalem will fall. He referred to the biblical record, stating that the City of Jerusalem will be utterly devastated. Its houses will be robbed and mass violence will ensue, including rape.

He said, "The first event predicted is a war against Jerusalem, in which all nations participate. In that war a part of the people in Jerusalem go into captivity, but the rest remain in the city." (12) He further believed this decimation would not only cover Jerusalem but the entire Palestine region, including the Gaza strip and the Trans-Jordan. (13)

Statements like the above in the 1940's, even among Christians, were considered radical. Today such concepts quickly draw ridicule. On the other hand, the idea of a world war in the Middle East is not inconceivable. In fact, in spite of current peace efforts, to some the question is not if, but when will there be a war in the Middle East?

Houteff also foresaw the mass Jewish exodus of 1947 and

1948. (13) His comments preceded the official recognition of Israel as a state in 1948. They preceded the Middle East war of 1967 and Kuwait's war with Iraq in 1991. Thus, he foresaw the Middle East conflict and its implications 45 years in advance.

The "Rod's" message strikes a stark contrast to various groups in Christendom who teach that Israel will defeat all her enemies. It predicts the opposite. For awhile, Israel may see success but face catastrophe sometime during that great war. Defeat will encompass the Arabic world, but will also include Israel's backers like the US.... A faithful few will remain and join God's kingdom which Houteff confidently believed would be established in the Promised Land after the devastation. Time alone will reveal the utter truth or nonsense of these prognostications. But, as we view current events, they give us pause.

This brings us to another aspect of present and future affairs. What did Houteff say would become of Communism? Interestingly enough, in 1941, long before the U.S.S.R. became a threat, before World War II he forecasted Communism's rise and its future hold on the world. In 1946, about a year after the close of World War II, he stated:

"And the world knows that labor and management are now engaged in their greatest struggle, and that as a result Communism threatens the whole world." (14)

In 1948, he said, "The world sees Communism as a hydra-headed monster behind a bush, and nations are already, so to speak, smiting their knees one against the other while they look at it. (10)

"The warring nations are already divided into two distinct ideological camps. On the one side are the democratic governments, while on the other side are the totalitarian. If the latter continue successfully to prosecute their relentless conquest for world-dominion and sovereignty, the only victorious way out for the Christian nations, as they humanly view their plight, will be to surrender their power to the church. For, Catholic set against Catholic, and Protestant against Protestant, in mortal combat, they will in dread fear be inspired to saddle the beast, and to re-establish the church as its driver in order to free themselves from the shackles of totalitarianism, and to safeguard Christianity. They will see victory in this stratagem, if it be denied them in war...

"Such a combination of circumstances will result in a replication of the international church-and-state rule of the Middle Ages, and will relegate to the scrap heap the world's finest instrument of human liberty—the divinely inspired Constitution of the United States of America...And what is more, a system that will, on pain of death for nonconformity, exact a form of worship in violation of the conscience, is anything but Democracy and Christianity...The church and state union will bring 'a time of trouble, such as never was since there was a nation.'" (15)

He also pointed out that this international order will be headed by two key persons—a larger-than-life charismatic figure who will be the voice and religious authority of Christendom, and a chief political despot, commonly termed among Christians as the "666."

Again in 1948, commenting on the seventeenth chapter of Revelation, he wrote:

"Communism being the only world-wide ruling power since the world began, to hate religion, the church, is itself solid proof that the ten horns are symbolical of Communism, and that the beast represents a period of time in which Communism is about to dominate the world seat of government." (16)

Simply put, the western world will lose out in "the greatest of all battles" in the Middle East. Communism will become the unexpected beneficiary of the world's political throne; although, now, Communism has met its demise. This threat of totalitarian rule will cause the West and Christendom to rally and form a one-world economic-religious-political machine—The New World Order.

The Berlin wall's collapse, dissolution of the Soviet Union, renewed freedom of Eastern Europe have all been touted as the definite sign that Communism is inoculated and the cold war over. It appears that Houteff's statements refer more to the staunch threat of Communism which arose after the 1950's but certainly not in the 1990's. Actually, in his writings, Houteff insisted that Communism would not die. Instead, it will appear "about to dominate the world seat of government." (16) It would appear that he was wrong on this account, but the story is not over.

On the other hand, he did not believe the "new world order" would be Communist, capitalist, democratic, Catholic or Protestant, but ecclesiastic—a church-state/religious-political system. This goose mixture, known to many Christians as "the image of the beast," weds all into mutual agreement. The following statement will help clear the picture.

"...All these facts show that though Communism appears to be the next power to rule the world, this symbolic prophecy points out that the world will next be ruled by an international religious system, by Babylon the Great...The Scarlet-colored beast [of Revelation chapter 17], therefore, is the symbol of the world government into which the United Nations will finally evolve." (17) [] Brackets ours.

In other words, Communism will voluntarily give up its right to rule and instead submit to a church-state system spawned and nurtured in the US. Such a phenomenon could only happen, Houteff pointed out, with an all inclusive church federation. Today, he probably would refer to it as the "Christian Coalition" or the "Moral Majority." Why will Communism step aside? This one world system will offer a remedy for the world's ills, a proposed utopia. Perhaps this will lure Communism into surrendering its political dominance.

There are others who would agree with Houteff and are unconvinced of Communism's relegation to antiquity and the cold war's end. They exhibit China, Vietnam, Southern Africa, Central and South America, Cambodia, North Korea, and others as examples. Communism, they insist, is a master of deception, retreating only to return in greater and deadlier force. They would not see Houteff's portrayal as impossible.

In his book, <u>You can Trust the Communists (to be Communists)</u>, Dr. Fred Swartz wrote:

"The Communist method of advance may be likened to the hammering of a nail. It is a very foolish person who brings the hammer down with a crashing, resounding blow and then keeps pushing. When the first blow has spent itself, back must go the hammer in preparation for the next blow...

"For those not trained in dialectical thinking, it is very difficult to understand that Communists have a fixed and changeless goal, but that their method of approach reverses itself all the time [as in hammering a nail]. The tendency is to judge where they are going by the direction in which they are moving." (19)

In 1982, Anatoli Golitsyn, a former KGB planner who defected to the USA, wrote a book about the Communist's long range plans for world conquest. The book, entitled, New Lies for Old, published in 1984, accurately predicted the liberating of the USSR, Eastern Europe, and tearing down the Berlin Wall, about six years before the events unfolded. Time permits short excerpts.

"Communists strategists are now poised to enter into the final offensive phase of their long-range policy...for the complete triumph of Communism.

"...Communist strategist are equipped in pursuing their policy, to engage in maneuvers and stratagems beyond the imagination of Marx or the practical reach of Lenin and unthinkable to Stalin. Among such previously unthinkable stratagems are the introduction of false liberalization in Eastern Europe and, probably, in the Soviet Union and the exhibition of spurious independence on the part of regimes in Romania, Czechoslovakia and Poland...demolition of the Berlin Wall might even be contemplated...The Communists have succeeded in concealing from the West that the non-Communist parties are secret partners, not alternatives or rivals and that the new power structures, though they have democratic form, are in reality more viable and effective structures introduced and guided by Communists parties with broader base. Because of this Communist control, they are not true democracies and cannot become so in the future." (20)

Whatever one may think of Houteff's teachings on current events, one must consider that he was not a lunatic or another religious zealot—His life may have been more than a stroke on the canvass of time, fading into the background. At least to Davidians, he was a brush guided by the hand of an All-knowing God, painting pictures of the world yesterday, today, and tomorrow.

Houteff's commentaries and forecasts of current and future

events were by far the least recognized aspect of his message. This was and is especially true in Adventists circles. When most Adventists think of "The Shepherd's Rod," fear and loathing envelops them. A bitter pungency palates their consciousness like tasting an acrid herb. Why? Strangely enough, most do not know. Sometimes, its because they have heard some repeated misconception and accepted it without question, especially if it came from a church leader. Perhaps the most common misconception is the idea that Davidians will literally slaughter all Seventh-day Adventists. An example of this was in the fall of 1993. Rumors reached Federal authorities in Washington that Davidians planned to bomb Adventist churches. Panic-stricken, Adventist pastors from Texas to the East coast warned their parishioners. Not all. Some church leaders chose not to cause alarm. Others alerted local police and endeavored to search or stop Davidians from attending church services. The author, himself, received a call from a reputable church member regarding this so-called bomb threat.

It was almost comical in a way. In another, it revealed deep-rooted problems and misunderstanding of the "Rod's" message. Nothing new. However, it hammered the point home. This particular misconception stems from one of Houteff's outstanding teachings. Biblically speaking, he believed that God's judgment or wrath falls first upon the SDA denomination, demonstrated in a physical slaying of Seventh-day Adventists, not by human hands but by God Himself, and His angels. Human beings have nothing at all to do with it. Not one statement from his pen or sermons have been found stating, implying, or inferring that humans will have any part in this slaying.

Apparently the misunderstanding is derived from the primary Bible passage used to describe this catastrophic event. It is found in the ninth chapter of the book of Ezekiel. There, the Old Testament prophet vividly portrays God's anger falling upon Jerusalem, the temple, and the entire kingdom of Judah. Non-participants in the "abominations," who instead mourned and cried out against the wrongs, were marked or sealed, allowing angels of death to spare them.

Houteff explained that this passage prefigured the Adventist denomination. Hence, Davidians believe that the physical slaying graphically portrayed, applied to our time not to Ezekiel's. He did write about ancient Jerusalem's destruction by the Babylonians, also a judgment from God. Houteff insisted that this was only the backdrop or type of the primary event—the judgment upon "Modern Israel." He believed that his view was supported from various Bible texts and from Mrs. E.G. White's writings, who wrote:

"Study the 9th chapter of Ezekiel. These words will be literally fulfilled." (21)

"Here we see that the church [the Adventist world church] the Lord's Sanctuary was the first to feel the stroke of the wrath of God." (22) [] Brackets ours.

One reason for such drastic measures is the fact that the denomination has become so tainted under the current order of things, it cannot adequately represent God, His love, and final plan for humanity. It is unfit, in its present condition, to complete the proclamation of true Christianity to an already skeptical world. Neither can God judge the world without first giving it indisputable evidence of His truth and character. Therefore, this slaughter is sometimes referred to as the purification of the church.

Without objective study of the subject one can easily see how misconceptions could occur. Mix in existing prejudice and fear and behold, a bomb threat! Besides, who wants to hear about judgment falling on them? Davidians may say that the denomination is in denial.

The interesting note here is, that neither Houteff nor fundamental "Rod" believers subscribe to the use of firearms. The author could find no evidence, proving otherwise. Mt. Carmel Center had no firearms of any sort. Residents may have believed in the right to bare arms, as set forth by the constitution, but did not themselves exercise that right.

Houteff not only wrote of doctrinal matters, as mentioned earlier. He also wrote of science, education, and health. It may be a good place here to mention one particular scientific prediction. While commenting on a passage in the book of Genesis, he wrote:

"...Astronomical science has discovered that in our solar system there are besides the planet Earth eight other planets depending on the sun for light, heat, and life-giving energy. (The probability is that three more planets will be discovered..." (23)

This statement was first published in 1940. Since that time, interestingly enough, some astronomers believe there are more planets yet to be discovered. (24) Recent findings seem to support the possibility.

Another out standing tenet of the "Rod's" message was its teaching on re-establishment of, what may be termed, God's Kingdom of Glory in the Holy Land. This teaching was, and still is, perhaps the most difficult for Adventists to swallow.

In typical Adventist theology, God's kingdom will not be established until the second coming of Christ. At which time, the saints will be changed to immortality, and transported to heaven for a thousand years of bliss. After which, they descend again to earth in the city of unsurpassed splendor, the "New Jerusalem." (25) The wicked will then be permanently

destroyed. Then all the saints from time immemorial will occupy a re-created earth for eternity. Houteff agreed with this fundamental doctrine but simply believed that before this God must begin His kingdom in the Holy Land.

This doctrine was, and is, a key feature of the "Rod." The basic concept being: What God intended to do through ancient Israel, He will finally accomplish today through spiritual Israel.

God intended to reveal His character through His people to all humanity. This could only be accomplished through a practical demonstration—a society of righteousness, perfect health, peace, and order—where God's methods are truly practiced. A society superior in every branch of social and scientific endeavor—far superior to anything mankind has yet seen. A kingdom made up of every race, kindred and people all living in one accord. That would be a witness, a testimony like no other. This, argued Houteff, must begin in the context of our present world filled with its problems and distress. Davidians argue that it would be the crowning effort on God's part to rescue mankind from perdition, the final and only solution to the world's ills. Houteff put it this way:

"Now when the world needs and longs for peace more than

ever before, God, who only is able to give it is loudly declaring that those who really want peace can have it if they but come to Him...When all God's servants as one 'arise and shine,' then a little one shall become a thousand, and a small one a strong nation. Then the saints will be quickly gathered and wickedness brought to an end. This is God's way of finishing the Gospel work...If we stand faithful to God's Word, we shall finally behold all these wonders and live for evermore." (26)

This kingdom will begin after the afore-mentioned slaying or purification and political upheavals. It will leave the church a group of super-Christians, referred to in Revelation as the 144,000. (27) Christians, such as we have never seen before, who will span the globe with the true gospel. Inviting all to become citizens of the Kingdom of God, they will usher in the very end of time. He continues:

"The kingdom (the church purified and apart from the world) is to be as natural and as real as was the kingdom of ancient Israel, but there will be no sinners in it...this kingdom shall be self-governing under theocracy." (28)

Not all will join this grand state. Yet, according to this view of Scripture, millions will join the kingdom. In fact, in some cases whole nations. In brief, the "Rod" was a kaleidoscope of biblical themes, pointing to a time when God will take the "reins in His own hands." (29) A great day for those who seek purity of heart and life. A terrible day for those do not, who must face the justice of the Creator.

Houteff's message was a description of events leading up to that day, what to expect when it arrived, and how to be prepared for it. It was sometimes referred to as "the 11th hour," or "great and dreadful day of the Lord," or "Judgment of the living"—the beginning of the end.

Descriptions like this may offend many, evoke pity from some, and spark deep reflection in others. Then there are those who, after careful study, have concluded that the Davidian message is the truth. Houteff, was not particular about who agreed with his message. He taught it as he saw it and worked untiringly for over twenty-five years to communicate it within Adventist circles. He was not boastful, proud, or arrogant about what he taught. However, he was congenially definitive and pointed when declaring what he believed was the Word of God. Houteff died believing, with absolute confidence, that one day his message would come to complete fulfillment. Not because he said it, but because he was certain that the Bible prophecies have not, and will not fail to materialize although not always according to man's timetable or according to man's plan.

Chapter 8

A Knock-Out Blow

In spite of Houteff's resolute efforts the tendency toward extremism grew.

By and large, most of the movement was not threatened. Most were not extremists. But two problems existed that laid the foundation for future disaster. First, there were those who sought notoriety, who, oftentimes, held strange or warped views. Second, many did not study the message carefully, but were content to place their conscience
in Houteff's hands. Subsequently, they developed a superficial knowledge of the Davidian message. They did not thoroughly understand its doctrines for themselves. Instead, they rode waves of fervor and enthusiasm.

Houteff consistently encouraged believers to study for themselves, to accept the Rod on a biblical basis. Because it was truth, not simply because he said it. He also strongly encouraged them to develop a deep personal relationship with God. On one hand you had those anxious to lead and on the other those vulnerable to deception.

Houteff was not caught off guard. He was certainly aware of the danger. In fact, he warned repeatedly about the dangers that faced the movement. Some of his later writings not only addressed the denomination, but members of the Association as well. In other words, he made a more general thrust with special warnings to Rod believers. It seemed as though he was preparing the movement for great adversity. He even accurately predicted the almost fatal strike. In 1951, years beforehand, he penned these prophetic words:

"Everything that can be done against God's message of today will be done...Unparalleled, therefore, is the urgency that every eleventh-hour church member [Rod believers or Davidians] now quickly and solidly brace himself against the Enemy's effort to deliver a knock-out blow. We must be alert, too, to realize that the blow is to come from surprisingly unsuspected foes—from professed friends of the gospel. . ." (1) Brackets added.

Long before 1951, Houteff sought to forestall this coming "blow". In 1946, he wrote:

"Even some present Truth believers [Davidians] now and then drop a word of criticism, saying things by which to bolster their own reputation and down another's or to win someone to their way of thinking at the expense of God's cause!" (2)

"Today as in Moses's day many are duplicating the sins of that people: Some are all on fire one day, and all on ice the next. . . .Still others are constantly trying to promote themselves by continual fault-finding against the ones that bear the whole burden of the load. So it is that there must be among us today—antitypical doubters, complainers, office seekers and faultfinders, admitting one great truth one day and forgetting it the next day-yet expecting to be sealed with the seal of God and to stand with the lamb on Mt. Zion!" (3)

"In the spiritual warfare," continues Houteff writing in 1944, "the Christian's Adversary does not nap. He, too, seeks his opportunity to break down their courage and morale and thus accomplish their defeat. . .We could expect his assault upon us [Davidians] to come from the place we least expect it. So, unless we know what our weakest spot is how could we know where the Devil is going to attack us?

"The enemy made Laodiceans [Adventist denomination] believe they have no need of more Truth, they have all Truth that is necessary to get them through Heaven's portals. . .Now we [Davidians] really are enriched with Truth if we have studied and assimilated what has been given us. . .Therefore the Devil is not going to attack us where he attacked Laodiceans, but he will tell us that we are poor in Truth." (4) Brackets added.

Violation of this warning propelled the movement into disillusionment. Davidia, since the passing of Victor Houteff, has been overwhelmed with one extreme or another. While the denomination is plagued with liberalism and complacency, Rod believing Adventists have been infected with fanaticism. Considering the Seventh-day

Adventist's mind-set, the Rod's message itself was based upon new concepts, but certainly not fanatical. Unpopular? Assuredly. Starling? Yes! Fundamental? Conservative? Definitely.

One of Houteff's most impassioned warnings was given on April 22, 1950. It was not only an entreaty but an accurate prediction of what was to befall the movement. Note that it was not only a direct counsel to Rod-believing Adventists, and denominational Adventists but in many respects it was a commentary on Christendom as a whole. It is necessary to recount an extended portion to convey full import.   "Miracle-mongers and Miracle-hunters, fanatics all, bear in mind, may become dangerously subversive, ready to sabotage everything that is not in accordance with their thinking. Loose and rattling tongues will endeavor to shake the faith of us all. The ones, though, who bear the heaviest burden of feeding the flock with 'meat in due season' will be the Devil's main targets. At just such a time as this, these devoted followers of God will profit most by the Lord's advice:

"'Trust ye not in a friend, put ye not confidence in a guide: keep the doors of thy mouth from her that lieth in thy bosom...'

"It will be discovered that there will be thousands of voices, some from professed believers, and some from those who fight against the faith of the saints, one voice condemning one thing, and another condemning another thing, and what one condemns, another will approve. But when held close to the light of God's word, all their discordant philosophizing and murmurings, their man-made plans and carnal ideas, will be seen to be but a tumult of envy, jealousy, pride, self-opinionation, hatred, malice, politics, greed, prejudice, and every other selfishness. These unfortunate, self-sent ones, being yet in spiritual darkness, doubtless imagine themselves to be working for God with zeal and energy. But one day they will horrifyingly discover that they have been working against the Lord, as Saul of Tarsus discovered about himself. May the prayers of the saints awaken them, and put them working for the Lord..." (5)

The reality is that these comments perfectly crystallized the turbulence that would overtake Rod believers as well as the theological battles that would confront the Adventist denomination. This phenomenon began just a few years after Houteff made these statements, beginning in the mid 1950's and persists today.

Although storms within Davidia did not surge until Houteff's death in 1955, gale winds already blew. Even as early as 1938 some sought power.

In the Summer of 1938, the Houteffs journeyed to Bulgaria for a few months, leaving E. T. Wilson, vice-president, in charge. Remember, Wilson was a former denominational worker and SDA Conference president, dismissed after embracing the Rod's message. M.J. Bingham, the Association's assistant editor, expert linguist and writer, tried to wrest authority from Wilson. Tension tightened as Bingham, in episodic fashion strove to convince Wilson to relinquish his position. Wilson's refusals only made matters worse. Apparently, a genuine Christian and a fine, nonpower-hungry leader, Wilson desired only to faithfully shoulder his responsibilities. Unfortunately, Bingham coveted more.

By the time the Houteffs' returned in the fall of 1938, the controversy escalated. Houteff quickly and decisively denounced Bingham's escapades and laid the matter to rest.

Houteff was well aware of Bingham's thirst for power. Later, Bingham's thirst of another kind surfaced when his numerous sexual liaisons were discovered. (5) This scandal and disgrace caused Bingham's prompt dismissal and eviction from the campus. After some time, and only after Bingham claimed repentance, Houteff allowed his return to the Center. He was not, however, to hold a leadership role.

On the heels of Houteff's death, in 1955, Bingham failed another attempt at leadership seizure. By 1965, he finally became leader of his own newly formed faction, the "Bashan Association" in Missouri.

Benjamin Roden was another individual who tried to grasp power. After Houteff's death, he too became the leader of his own faction. This faction is now known to the world as the "Branch Davidians", later headed by Vernon Howell, a.k.a. David Koresh. A brief glimpse of Roden, before Houteff's death and establishment of the Branch group, highlights elements and personalities that eventually splintered the movement.

Roden, a radical member of the Association, came to Mt. Carmel Center during the Summer of 1946. An incident, during worship at an Adventist church in Odessa, Texas, exemplified his radical nature in overdrive. Having been identified as Rod-believing Adventists, Roden and company were barred entrance.

Albeit it was not uncommon for Rod believers to be barred, and in some cases physically accosted. Roden was no newcomer to this kind of treatment. Normally, Davidians simply waited outside until the service ended or tried attendance at another church. Roden and his companions decided to do something different. As the service progressed, they unscrewed the doors from their hinges and entered the church. Roden's wife locked herself in one of the rooms and refused to leave, creating quite a stir. (5)

Fanatical behavior was not altogether out of character for Roden. It was out of character for what the Davidian message portrayed, and it did not set well with Houteff.

These and similar events deeply disturbed him. So much so, it became quite obvious at times. In the last few years of his life, he did less and less public speaking. Instead, he allowed others to speak. (5) In addition, his health deteriorated. Constant stress and long hours took their toll. His heart weakened, and he was hospitalized periodically. In 1952, he suffered a stroke which affected his right side. Afterwards, he walked with a cane and noticeable limp but otherwise remained unaffected.

The work load further exacerbated his condition. He assisted various departments daily, did much of his writing at night, awoke early every morning for public devotions and the day's regular activities. (5) All this, topped with spiritual concerns and confronting various problems daily, no doubt, contributed to his failing health. Increasing fanatical, misguided elements compounded his already stressful responsibilities. Despite the presence of department heads and managers, Houteff's involvement was necessary in almost every aspect of the Association. The movement's constant growth demanded his personal attention.

In 1953, Houteff launched what became known as the "hunting campaign," producing major changes in Adventist outreach. During the late 1930' and through the 1940's, the Association emphasized mailing millions of pieces of free literature to SDA's world-wide, a.k.a. the "fishing campaign." Fitting terms since the literature acted as bait, arousing interest. (7) Some Adventists, desirous of studying the Rod's message, would not openly declare interest. The literature, coming to their homes allowed them privacy of action.

The "hunting" campaign sent an army of workers to Adventist homes. (7) In this way, they clinched any interest sparked by the literature. To facilitate travel, the Association purchased a new fleet of Chevrolets. Workers drove across-country visiting thousands of SDA homes. Reaching just over 800,000 Seventh-day Adventists world-wide was the Association's goal.

Imagine the extensive work and expense involved in conducting this endeavor. Houteff himself describes the feeling best. On November 26, 1954, in what is believed to have been his last sermon, he stated:

"Why must the message bearers come to your door in order to bring the message to you? Because, as you already know, most of the ministers have closed the church doors and the laity's minds and hearts against the Lord's message for today. . . .Here you are plainly told that in the gathering time the servants of God are compelled first to fish His people, then to hunt them.

Since our first contact with them has been through the literature, it, therefore, must be the fishing. Rightly so, too, because as it is scattered everywhere as the leaves of autumn. . . Now, however, we are in the hunting period, and we have already begun to hunt them, be they in the city or in the country, in places easy to get to, or in places hard to get to. Wherever they live, there they must be hunted. . ." (7)

The 1950's brought more startling announcements and trends. In September, 1954, Houteff made the most stunning declaration of all. The Association would sell Mt. Carmel Center. The move was a fund-raiser for the hunting campaign, a climactic endeavor to reach the denomination. Houteff portrayed the prevailing sentiments:

"The hunting Campaign launched last year initiated and heralded a new electrifying and progressive advancement of present Truth.

"Now again, with even greater emphasis toward reaching her goal, Mount Carmel Center makes the following announcement to all faithful Davidians who will realize that this good news is perhaps nothing short of a sign. Mount Carmel Center, by commencing to first sell its excess property, then the whole. . ." (8)

As stated above, the objective was to sell the property to acquire funds for an "all-out effort" to reach the Denomination. Most surprising was the plan to sell all, "the whole." (8) The December newsletter, reiterated this unprecedented move.

"The sale of Mt. Carmel property was pictured as being a move that should awaken all to the fact that the eleventh-hour Message is on the very verge of a final and all-out effort to reclaim the church from the hands of the tare-sower." (9)

To earn the most from the sale, the property was sub-divided into smaller lots. Another newsletter put it this way. "Be it, therefore, known that part of Mount Carmel property is being subdivided for high class residences beginning at the old peach orchard near Mount Carmel entrance." (10) With city limits moving onto Association's property, it was the right time to sell.

Whether Houteff knew the movement had reached its zenith was unknown. Yet, he did know it would suffer a time of extreme perplexity. In his last sermon, he uttered astonishing words indelibly etched in the minds of his audience. "Mt. Carmel", he said, "will wither and die before Ezekiel nine and we will not be able to depend on one soul but Christ. . .Husband apart, wife apart, weeping between the porch and the altar." (5)

Houteff was not to see Mt. Carmel Center reach her goal, nor his own prediction of its disintegration. He was not to behold the coming disasters that would almost crush the work to which he had given his all for over 25 years.

By January of 1955, about a month after making this startling statement, he was admitted to the Hillcrest Hospital of Waco for heart problems. This time would be his last visit.

Since early 1954 his health had worsened. One account said he actually looked "green." (5) It has also been reported that doctors said that he literally had holes in his heart. They were astonished that he had lived so long. In spite of his grave illness, some Davidians concluded that he would never die. A concept unproven from his writings, his sermons, or from testimonies of those who knew him. On the contrary, he publicly rebuffed those who dared to teach such an idea. (5) Like other founders, he had hoped he would live to see the fruition of his labors. He had desired that his work would reach completion in a few short years. (11) He did not set dates or claim that he was anything more than a messenger. He believed final authority always rested with God. If the message was truth, it would, sooner or later, meet success. (12)

On the night of February 4, with his wife and another member, a registered nurse, by his side, he waved one of his booklets in the air. "This is very important for God's people", he declared. For some time members had known that he had been involved in the study of a particular Bible prophecy that had significance to the future of the movement. It was believed to have been a study of a forty-two month prophecy found in the Old Testament book of Daniel, and also Revelation. The booklet has been identified as Volume Two, number 15, of his "Timely Greetings" series. (5)

When his wife impatiently asked, "What is it?. . .Tell us", He simply responded, "I'll tell you in the morning". Since they expected his release the next morning, this convinced them to wait. In a few hours they would finally know what had so deeply impressed his mind the past months.

It was not to be. The next morning, assisted by a hospital nurse, he returned to his bed, laid back, and breathed his last. Victor Tasho Houteff, passed away on Saturday morning, February 5, 1955, less than one month before his 70th birthday. His heart refused to give another beat.

On that memorable morning, the sun arose as on any other day. The world may have appeared the same to most of Waco's residents. To Davidians, the sky was brass; to them, nothing would ever be the same. Few, no doubt, remembered Houteff's words of caution to help them withstand the coming, crippling blow. None, even if they had remembered, could have imagined how it would come, and how much it would alter their lives.

February 5, 1955, brought consternation and disappointment to Davidians everywhere. Most were dumbfounded! Although Houteff had suffered serious illness for sometime, many refused to accept the possibility of his death. They believed God would not allow it. Who would be the new leader? What direction would the work take, now? How would they go on? Unknown to them, Houteff's death was the incipience of the swing that delivered the nearly fatal wound to Davidia.

Mourners, nationwide, attended his funeral. Mt. Carmel Chapel proved too small for the occasion. Instead, the service was held in the larger, newly constructed publishing building. (12) Even local businessmen came. Apparently, Houteff was respected and well known throughout Waco for his business skills and integrity. It was said that his reputation was such that all you needed to purchase on credit was to mention Mt. Carmel Center. (5)

While Houteff lived, some believers became his closest friends. To others, he, and the movement became their greatest foe. They were disappointed or embittered by one of several things. It may have been the messages' strict demands on their lifestyles, and Houteff's unflinching adherence to them. Institutional living, such as that at the Center, can easily create disaffection. Some viewed Houteff and the Association as inflexible. He was never rude or gruff, but his frank, no nonsense approach offended certain members. Others were wounded by alienation and ostracism from friends and family for having embraced the Rod's teachings in the first place. Of this class, some denied the message and opposed the Association's work

On the other hand, many practically worshipped Houteff (perhaps subconsciously). They saw Houteff not the Scriptural messages he bore. To this group, his death was truly a bitter draft. It appears that this class, more than any other, coupled with the fanatical fringe, eventually propelled the movement into a tailspin.

All agreed on one thing, Houteff was a remarkable man. As they viewed his face for the last time, most Davidians agreed that he was the modern-day counterpart of the ancient prophet Elijah. He was God's prophet for the Eleventh-hour of Earth's history. Although disappointed, they decided to continue the work he started.

Merritt W. Wolfe, Bible instructor, remarked in the committal sermon, observations that crystallized their thoughts. "Brother Houteff, our leader, was not a quitter; he did not permit himself to be overcome by discouragement. Neither did he give himself over to feelings. If he were to speak to us Davidians upon this occasion, today, I am sure he would tell us, 'on with the work. Stop nothing short of victory.' He would admonish us 'do not repeat the same mistakes of Israel in the past, or that of modern Israel, by stopping where their leaders went to rest. Keep on going; do not stop just because I am resting. Keep on going; look to the Lord, the Author and Finisher of your faith.'" (12)

Davidia's leadership did not succumb to "modern Israel's" (Adventist denomination) mistakes, as most Adventists assumed. They slid into "ancient Israel's" pitfalls locked within the deadly embrace of extremism. Why do we keep repeating this fanaticism theme? Simply put, it was this that Houteff fought so vigorously. After his death, it was this that overtook Davidia and delivered the "knock out blow". Albeit, the blow did not come suddenly. It waited seven years.

After his death, Florence Houteff informed the Council that her husband had suggested that she take leadership. A suggestion unconfirmed to this day. Some believed she had wanted leadership, and they question what had really transpired. Others accepted her statement. Some prominent Adventists rumored that Houteff appointed his wife to be his successor. No evidence backs their conclusion.

Whether Houteff recommended her or not, she did seem the best choice. Capable. Talented. Respected. Possessing intricate knowledge of the message and the Association's operation, she had been close to him in every aspect of the work.

Davidia confirmed her succession and elected her Chairman

of the Executive Council. However, she would not hold the office of President. She would fill the position as Vice-president. Davidians adhere to the biblical basic that the Association's president is one directly called of God. Not being viewed as a prophet as Victor Houteff had been, Florence Houteff could not have held presidential office.

The Council, led by Florence Houteff, continued to sell the property. Houteff had sold about 35 acres just prior to his death. By June, 1956, the Council had sold all but 18 of the original 375 acres. (13) Rapid encroachment of city limits compelled the Council to sell the property in larger tracts. Strangely, they did not place the funds into the hunting work, as Houteff planned. Instead, in March 1957, they purchased 941 acres in Elk, Texas about ten miles from Waco. They built another facility, moved their entire operation there, and named it "The New Mt. Carmel Center."

Please note: that it was at this site, years later, the Branch Davidians would establish their headquarters.

In 1956, Davidian leadership formulated additional interpretations on the aforementioned 42 month biblical prophecy. (18) Apparently the idea was sparked by Houteff's statement that the booklet he waved in his hand the night before he died was "very important to God's people." Knowing of Houteff's involvement in a new study prior to his death, the Council concluded that the 42 month prophecy, particularly Revelation chapters 10 and 11, qualified as that study. Yet, no one really knew the subject of his study or the conclusions he had reached.

Traditionally, Adventists teach that the 42 months or 3 1/2 years or 1260 days (reckoning 30 days to a month) represent 1260 years in prophetic time. (14) (15) (16) Events during the middle ages, 538 AD to 1798 AD, fulfilled this prophecy. Victor Houteff also taught this traditional Adventist view. (17) But the new Davidian leadership claimed that the prophecy had a dual meaning, referenced to actual days not prophetic years. They set its fulfillment from November 5, 1955 to April 22, 1959. They decreed that Houteff's death cued the beginning or approach of the 42 month period. Since he died in February, 1955. No one knows why November 5 was chosen as the starting date.

What did the Council expect to happen after April 22, 1959? According to various letters, documents, articles, and interviews, they expected several major events:

- The world's religions to unite against Communism.
- The terrible judgment of God described in Ezekiel chapter nine, whereby all unfaithful Adventists (including Davidian Adventists) would be physically destroyed leaving only a 144,000 faithful.
- That a world war would occur in the Middle East.
- That God would establish a Kingdom in the Holy land.

These skewed teachings traumatized the movement and placed its entire ministry on the chopping block. Credibility and over 25 years of work would stand or fall on fulfillment of these predictions. 1956 through 1959 thrust the work onto a thin track with unprecedented speed.

For example, in the Spring of 1957, the leadership started a national radio program. Dudley Goff, Davidian minister and field worker, was speaker. Mixed with this dab of extraneous teachings, the outside world heard the Rod's message for the first time.

Houteff always focused primarily on the SDA denomination. With the exception of one or two interviews, he never used the media. He never set dates, exact or approximate. (19) He did not conduct sign campaigns or distribute literature en masse. The new order had no such reservations.

Throughout the summer of 1957, Davidians worked SDA camp meetings across the country. They distributed literature, displayed signs on cars or busses, reading, "Hear ye the Rod". (20)

In June, 1958, they published an open letter to the 48th Quadrennial World Session of the General Conference of Seventh-day Adventists, convened in Cleveland, Ohio. The letter outlined key points of their message and pled for Session delegates' acceptance. At that session, where thousands of Adventists gathered, Davidians distributed more literature, conducted another sign campaign on cars, busses, in Hotel lobbies, and held lectures. (20)

Most Davidians seemed in agreement with the new interpretations and predictions. However, a sizable group questioned Mrs. Houteff and her colleagues.(5) This conservative class was uneasy with the Council's decisions. They saw disaster ahead. But their warnings and pleas drowned in the swell of majority expectations. Fanaticism finally overran the movement. Davidia was sucked into the eye of disappointment's storm.

A pivotal year proved to be 1959 when leadership waxed even bolder. In February, the Council made a startling announcement in another open letter this time addressed to the General Conference Committee. "By this letter", wrote the Council, "we make it known to you that we are now leaving this entire matter with the Lord to demonstrate whether He is leading in the work at Mt. Carmel, or whether He is leading you to stop your ears to the message which Mt. Carmel has put forth in her official publications. This means that The Shepherd's Rod message is now on the altar. If you are positive in your position that The Shepherd's Rod is not of the Lord and that your are being led of God to resist it, you will not hesitate to put your all on the altar as well. . . .Mt. Carmel hereby serves notice that she now leaves the prophecy of Revelation 11 as the Code has explained it, as the test by which the Lord will demonstrate whom He is leading." (21)

"Mt. Carmel believes the prophecy of Revelation 11 just as it has been published in The Symbolic Code—that we are in the forty-two months and are very near the end of them. . .That we have come to the time when all in the church must make their decision individually that will determine their eternal destiny.

"Mt. Carmel further believes that the forty-two months will end sometime this Spring that following their end war will be declared on the Two Witnesses by Christendom; that it will result in the death of the Two Witnesses; that they shall be dead for 3 1/2 days after which they shall be raised and exalted; that in this same hour the earthquake and slaying by the Lord will take place; and that the land [The Holy Land] will be ready, and the Kingdom be ushered in." (22) Brackets added.

So confident, so sure that what they predicted would occur, they without trepidation, placed the message "on the altar" of sacrifice - Davidia, the offering—the oblation. But fate held the knife. If the predictions failed, Houteff and the entire movement would be blamed even though he had never taught the new doctrines nor set dates. Years of untiring effort would be consumed in a firestorm of incredulity. How and why Mrs. Houteff and associates reconciled their new position in light of what Houteff had taught is an enigma. The media was alerted Davidian's had challenged the SDA denomination and the world. Outside Adventist circles, this was just another extremist group making a fool of itself.

The SDA denomination, may have viewed it as a giant leap toward winning Davidians back to the "fold". Surely after their predictions failed, most would publicly renounce Davidian theology and return to their local Adventist churches' status quo. Perhaps they thought a great disappointment would end a persistent, Davidian plague, rid them of this nagging foe. Some possibly suffered apprehension, thinking, What if Davidians were right? Others may have considered the whole affair nonsense. Whatever the reasons Church leaders never responded to the Davidian's challenge.

In March, 1959, the Council issued a call for "all who were in complete harmony with the message and Mt. Carmel's leadership to come to Mt. Carmel for the purpose of gathering in solemn assembly ...your presence," here reflects your belief in its validity." (21) As April 22 approached, they came from everywhere. They expected, shortly after that date, to see the confederation of Christian churches. The federation of Western nations. A world war in the middle East. The slaughter of unfaithful SDA's. The liberation and transportation of the 144,000 to Palestine to witness the first stage of God's eternal kingdom of peace.

Nearly 1,000 believers came to Mt. Carmel Center in the Spring of 1959. Most had relinquished everything—literally all their life possessions. They believed they stood on the kingdom's doorstep. They staked their hopes, their future on Davidia's predictions. They were not sure precisely when events would occur, but they were convinced it would be soon, very soon. Thomas Turner, "Central Texas Bureau of the News", put it this way:

"By the hundreds they arrived, everywhere: whole families and individuals, poor people and rich. Some wore clean but faded work clothes and came by bus. Most, however, were well-dressed, literate, driving cars of every type.

"There were babies and grandmothers; carpenters and farmers; professional men and typical teenagers. They had received the word to dispose of all their worldly possessions and report forthwith to Mount Carmel. . .They obeyed seemingly without question. . ." (23)

The "Waco Times Herald", reported interesting personal accounts of some who attended the Davidian sessions. One account reads, "'We were living in Calif., when we received the notice to assemble in Waco,' Tommy Thompson, a lean weather-beaten man in his 60's recalled, 'I owned a trenching machine business. After we received the notice we sold the business, our house and furniture. We packed the rest of our belongings—our bedding and cooking utensils—in the car and rented a trailer and brought them with us'" Thompson and his wife lived in a tent at the New Mt. Carmel Center. (24)

George Walton brought his wife, son, and 30 to 35 members from California. Walton, a former City of Los Angeles Board of Education employee, burned his bridges and lived in a tent. Mr. and Mrs. C.C. Lyons of Portland, Oregon sold their home and came to the Center. Because of Mr. Lyons's heart condition, they occupied an apartment at the Center. (24) The list goes on. Every state in the US and Canada was represented. (25)

Davidian leaders held meetings April 18—22, preparing believers for the anticipated events. Obviously, most Rod believers did not move to the Center. They were not confident enough in the leadership's conclusions to part with material possessions, travel to Waco, risking financial loss and embarrassment. Although, they may have supported them otherwise. Many accepted the "Shepherd's Rod" theological position, but rejected new interpretations of the 42 month prophecy. They adopted a watch and see attitude.

By adding their own ideas, Davidian conservatives felt that, their leaders added ignominy to the message and betrayed the movement. These conservatives accepted no deviation from the original teachings of Victor Houteff in exchange for what they termed, suppositions and "uninspired interpretations of Scripture." Their pleading and their attempts to halt the thundering tide of expectations failed. They would play a vital part in preserving the message and its work for the future. However, in 1959, conservatives prepared for the worst. A few remembered Houteff's forecast of the movement's turbulent future. Precisely how and when it would come, they could not tell. But they knew it would come, and they braced themselves.

The thrust, that delivered this near fatal blow, materialized after April 22 came and went uneventfully. The possibility of Victor Houteff's resurrection on or about that date had been discussed. (26) No meetings were held for about ten days. On May 3, 1959, an open-to-the-public meeting was called. (27) Other than a reaffirmation of their previous conclusions, information on that meeting is sketchy. Some members sensed a "feeling of desperation, of panic" within the group despite a calm outward appearance. An astute observation, confirmed by the fact that "only about two-thirds of the original number were present and attending meetings." (27) Yet, overall, these Davidians remained resolute, awaiting their expectation's fulfillment.

As May closed, they were pursued by perplexity and haunted by various ideas. Perhaps they had made William Miller's mistake. That forerunner of Seventh-day Adventism had discovered a prophetic date but had misunderstood the predicted event? Maybe they had made a miscalculation, also? Perhaps their predictions would meet fulfillment a few months later than expected? Undaunted by bombarding questions, they expressed confidence in their position.

On June 20, in an effort to lift the shroud of disappointment, a letter drafted by Mrs. Houteff, was read to the congregation. A portion of which encapsulated their mind-set and rationale. "Even some of us here", penned Mrs. Houteff, "if not all of us, in one way or another are not ready. . . . And if we are tempted to be impatient because the Lord does not see fit to bring to pass His prophesied events precisely when we think He should, let us consider again that our own fate might not be the desirable one were we now brought face to face with the great challenge of our loyalty to God.

"At any rate, if we as individuals have sincerely prayed that God would lead us individually and as a body, then we cannot conclude otherwise than that our present circumstance is according to His will. In view of this fact none will be so foolish as to act impetuously through disappointment. Instead all will quietly wait on the Lord for Him to make the next move or indicate what He would have us do now." (28)

Sunday, June 21, four representatives from the Denomination sought an audience with the Davidians. (28) (29) One had been appointed to represent the General Conference of SDA's, Mr. A. V. Olson, a past Vice President of the General Conference. Their mission was indeed unusual. Their purpose? Reclaim Davidians. (29) Davidian officials offered the four unlimited use of their tabernacle. (29) They recognized a ripe opportunity to witness. Could it be that after years of fiercely persecuting Rod believers, the denomination's leaders came to Waco, seeking them out devoid of political posturing? Obviously, they sensed Davidian's vulnerability. Victor Houteff was dead and hope in Davidian leaders was tattered. However, convincing believers to renounce the Rod would not be an easy task.

From June 24 to July 7, sixteen meetings were conducted. Davidians did not budge. The difficulty lay in counteracting the original "Rod" within biblical parameters using traditional Adventist theological context. They later agreed that seven representatives from both groups would meet at SDA General Conference Headquarters in Washington DC, to discuss "The Shepherd's Rod." The General Conference (G.C.) hoped this second meeting would reclaim Davidians.

Meetings began cordially, July 27. Davidians held to their convictions as firmly as they had in the previous series of meetings. Reports of the hearings revealed Conference leader's methods of refuting Davidian theology. Based almost exclusively on Mrs. White's writings, they quoted Houteff's statements that appeared to contradict her's. (30) This was the Denomination's customary practice. Davidians were blasted with numerous statements from Mrs. White's pen declaring the folly of time setting. While presenting Houteff's original teachings, Davidian logic sparkled in the light of biblical-Adventist theology. When they presented the additional interpretations, their logic lost its luster and pungence. On August 7, the meetings ended. General Conference leaders and Davidians would never again meet in such a capacity.

Glued to their theological position, Davidians had done their best to forewarn their own church. Yet, they could not explain why their predictions had failed. All attempts led them down untried roads, paths of no return. They shifted focus from Seventh-day Adventists to the Protestant population at large. They published booklets designed for a more general audience. Their nationwide radio broadcast, on the ABC network, was a key medium in presenting their message to a new audience. (29) They offered Bible study courses. Davidian leaders even encouraged visits to other churches, attendance at Sunday worship services and prayer meetings. (31) A strange practice for seventh-day Sabbath-keepers.

This new direction, however, only exacerbated the Davidian dilemma. For a time there was a bounty of Protestant interest. Even professors of theology used "Rod" material for their lectures. (32) Interest soon diminished. The "Rod's" message, based on fundamental Adventism, explained obscure and difficult Bible prophecies within that context. In other words, "The Shepherd's Rod" was designed for Seventh-day Adventists.

Protestants had long questioned some fundamental SDA beliefs. Beliefs that once classified Seventh-day Adventists as a cult. Seventh-day Adventism endured estrangement from Christendom for much of its existence, garnering understanding only in recent church history. As the denomination altered some peculiar views, it won acceptance into the family of evangelical churches, however slowly. Many ministries within Adventism neither welcomed nor accepted this liberal trend. They maintained fundamental positions. True

Davidians ranked in this group.

To avert difficulty with their audience, the new Davidian leadership altered and/or down-played long-standing Adventist beliefs. (32) This trend began at their first special session, September 24 - 29, 1961. (32)

By January 1962, they had discarded key features of the "Rod." (33) Unable to explain the failure of their predictions, they were drowning in doubts. Piece by piece, they dismantled Adventism, starting with "The Shepherd's Rod." Although they did not question their integrity, Davidian leaders denied that Ellen White and Victor Houteff were inspired, . (33)

Finally, in February, 1962, it all came crashing down. Davidian leadership rejected everything Adventist. They called a second, special session and announced their resignation. "All who came to Mt. Carmel in 1959 came because of their own decision to participate in the test." said the leaders. ". . . But the failure of the expected events to occur at that time showed there was something wrong with the 'Rod.'. . .Since as we view it, "the 'Rod' is not in harmony with the Bible, we are now serving notice that the Executive Council members will tender our resignations, to take effect as of the time of its reading in the Session. For we do not believe that Ezekiel 4 has a commission to either this Association or Mt. Carmel Center. Neither do we believe that Mrs. White had authority to apply Ezekiel 9 to the future when the Bible does not do so. . . ." (34)

At that second session, as promised, they further stated: "During the seven years that have since passed, we have directed and defended the Association with diligence according to our honest convictions of what constituted our duty. As long as we believed in all the teachings of the 'Rod' per se, we patiently bore the personal cost of being victimized by a constant stream of suspicion, slander, libel, and the many other unpleasant experiences that came in the line of duty. . .There is no alternative open to us but to resign since as we view it, so vital a change in the basic doctrines is involved that it leaves the Association without its declared prophetic commission. . .but since we do not now believe the Bible supports those teachings, we therefore are not qualified longer to head up the Association. The destiny of the Association rests entirely in the hands of the membership now." (35)

This resignation was read at the session's opening, March 11, 1962. They could not face the congregation. They had departed three days earlier and had left legal dissolution of the Association in the hands of a lawyer. After 25 years' ardent labor, the work of Davidians crashed and burned. It was over. What bitter disappointment? What humiliation? Many had sold their homes and all material goods and had awaited consummation of God's kingdom. Instead of entering the gates of bliss, they reentered a hostile world. What would they do? How would they erase so many years of their lives? How would they ever forget the movement that had been profoundly etched into their consciousness? Painful though it was, members tried putting Davidia behind them. They dashed into the future and hoped the past would not catch up.

Davidia scattered in retreat. Some publicly renounced the "Rod's" message, in their local congregations, and were welcomed back into full denominational fellowship. Others joined different denominations. A significant number escaped into the secular world, melting in so well, it was almost impossible to know they were ever affiliated with Davidians.

Although they left their faith in the Davidian movement, the movement never really left them. Somehow, an indelible mark remains. (5) This point was forcibly made with conservatives who did the opposite of their counterparts. Instead of removing themselves from the Davidia, they reorganized the work as close to the original as possible. Adhering to Victor Houteff's teachings and methods, they set no dates and made no predictions. They raised the movement from the wreckage of fate. They insisted that the original message was truth. Mistakes were made by the post- Houteff leadership. "The movement was knocked out, but not dead," they said, "only unconscious for a time." The church and the world had not heard the last of Davidians. These determined believers were convinced that Bible prophecies, as taught by Victor Houteff, would one day come to pass.

Between July 28 and August 7, 1961, a large group of conservatives reorganized in Los Angeles, CA. Thus began another association in fidelity to the original doctrines. On December 18, 1963, it was incorporated. (36)

Some conservatives did not immediately link themselves with this new organization in California, but remained aloof for years. Convinced that Houteff's message was true, they watched to see how the newly formed work would proceed. They were cautious. Others were confused, suspicious, traumatized, and hesitant to commit themselves to any organization. In time, they flowed with the main stream.

Thomas Turner, of the "Central Texas Bureau of The News", was right when he wrote: "It might not be altogether accurate to say that the end did come for the Davidians. Those familiar with the calm, deep zeal of its faithful will not be surprised at the news, one of these days, of a new Mount Carmel, complete with interpretations of Scriptural passages which have puzzled scholars for centuries."

Chapter 9

Can It Happen Again?

An ancient Near East proverb says: "You will never reach Mecca, I fear: for you are on the road to Turkestan". (1) Could it happen again? Is it possible that what happened with the Branch Davidian Seventh-day Adventists could be repeated? The Answer depends on our understanding of what took place near Waco, before, and during the fateful 51-day siege. In previous chapters we reviewed what led up to the infamous siege. We saw the tragedy's making, but can we prevent another Waco?

It is not only the dead Federal agents or the fiery end of Koresh and his followers that haunt us. It is also the controversy over who shot first? Who started the fire? Why federal agents did not delay the raid? What it tells us about ourselves is perhaps most disquieting. It reveals our vulnerability and our inability to appreciatively understand the human physchy. This disaster forces us to admit that we understand little about the phenomenon of religion. We seem to understand something of the workings of the human anatomy, but little of human capacity to believe.

The question is often asked, how could educated, intelligent people accept and unquestionably devote their lives to one man to the point of death? It is actually no different than what happened in the first century AD. When over 900 Jews of the Sicarii sect took their own lives and the lives of their loved ones at the Masada fortress rather than surrender to the Roman army. Perhaps it is no different than asking what happened in Guyana, South America, when under the leadership of Jim Jones, approximately the same number committed suicide? Is it unlike what occurred in Germany when one man, Hitler, led a nation into one of the greatest calamities of history?

Deciphering what took place at Branch headquarters is onerous enough much less finding a solution. Forthright examination of ourselves appears to tell us that it is unlikely that we will be able to prevent another Koresh, or another confrontation with nonconformists. History does not let us conclude otherwise.

   To begin answering the question is to try understanding what took place. Something this chapter or book cannot altogether do. It may unearth the root causes and provide a possible solution.

   So what happened? Some would say that the answer is simple. Koresh was deluded. He deceived his followers, and caused the death of over 80 people, including innocent children and government officials. Authorities did their best under the circumstances. Others do not accept this description. They say that the Government murdered Branch believers. One principal advocate of this scenario is Linda Thompson, a lawyer who produced convincing video footage of what appeared to be Federal agents shooting first on February 28, and the ATF starting the fire on April 19. "The word 'Waco' has become synonymous with two opposing scenarios", says Carol Moore, of the Committee for Waco Justice, "To many Americans —and especially authorities—it means crazed religious fanatics arming themselves to make war on the US government and committing mass suicide when they lose the war.

   "However, to other Americans, 'Waco' means a questionable, clearly illegitimate or even vicious and murderous government destruction of a dissident group." (2)

   Those who share these views, generally agree that there is a growing impatience and hence a definite aim at eradicating non-conformists groups particularly armed ones. In their ardent zeal to shut-down the radical citizenry, constitutional freedoms, rights and privileges are either overlooked, ignored, or deliberately rent. This leads to excessive force and a broken line between law enforcement and genocide. What happened in Philadelphia in the 1985 fire that killed eleven members of the MOVE group and destroyed two city blocks while law enforcement officers tried to make an arrest, is cited as an example.

   Another is Randy Weaver who retreated to rural Idaho with his wife, four children, and a family friend. Weaver and his friend, Kevin Harris, were wounded by Marshals. His son Samuel was shot in the back and killed, his wife Vicki and baby were killed by agents while standing in the doorway of their cabin. Weaver and Harris claimed that Federal agents ambushed them outside their home, after police shot and killed their dog. Not knowing who shot the dog, they returned fire. US Marshall, William Degan, was killed in the gun battle. Nine days later Weaver and Harris surrendered. These and other incidents are cited as evidence of the violent and aggressive trend of law enforcement. The Branch Davidian raid was just as blatant, but had more disastrous results.

"The Committee for Waco Justice", says Moore, "believes the facts already available provide compelling evidence that BATF and the FBI, through a combination of negligence and arrogance bordering on intentionality, did indeed massacre the Branch Davidians. No matter how the April 19th fires started, those who gassed Mount Carmel Center and rammed it with military tanks ultimately are responsible." (2)

In reference to various charges against Koresh and his group, such as, child abuse, sex with minors, illegal weapons, and polygamy the Committee and others asserted that the government had weak cases, and in some instances no evidence.

Dr. Gordon Melton, for example, made this alarming statement to the American Academy of Religion panel on the Branch Davidians, "As I examined the evidence of all the horrible things that Koresh had allegedly done, those horrible things began to melt away, they were unsubstantiated charges from witnesses who were biased and whose credibility was very low. The various accusations made had no foundation in fact. . .The question shifted to why did the government misuse its power in such a horrendous way?" (3)

Allegation of child abuse is one example. The Texas Department of Human Services employees including at least one social worker, made three visits along with McLennan County Sheriff's deputies. The department's summary of their investigation was succinct: "None of the allegations could be verified. The children denied being abused in any way by adults in the compound. They denied any knowledge of other children being abused. The adults consistently denied participation in or knowledge of any abuse to children. Examinations of the children produced no indication of current or previous injuries." (4)

Dr. Bruce Perry who interviewed children who were released during the siege, commented: "The term they used was 'Christian discipline'. . .Discipline is not abuse." (5)

It is accepted that Koresh had sex with girls under eighteen which may not be illegal under Texas law. National statutory rape laws are obscure and cumbersome to enforce, largely because of wide-scale promiscuity. The age of consent in Texas in 1993 was 14, if the girl was promiscuous, and 17 if she was not. In Koresh's case, he was viewed as a religious icon. Sexual relations with him was considered an honor, implied mutual consent, and posed a mountain for prosecutors to climb in court. Of course, no one agrees that sex with minors is either wise or morally correct.

Koresh's arms build-up was questionable, but not clearly illegal. Purchases were accepted as legal, at least as far as law enforcement officials were concerned. The problem resided primarily with "intent". The ATF suspected that he may have purchased legal firearms and parts but intended to use them to construct illegal weapons. Accusations difficult to prove since most government witnesses, were disaffected, former believers with questionable credibility. Little hard evidence existed to prove Koresh's intent. Paul H. Blackman, Ph.D., in his report, said "the Branch Davidians were using the explosive materials for construction projects and for refilling ammunition, both legal uses." (6) ATF officials decided to use their sparse evidence to obtain a search warrant. They anticipated uncovering solid proof and convicting the Branch group on weapons charges.

On February 28, 1993, Koresh told KRLD radio, "I'm a polygamist. Which is not according to your laws, I understand that, but according to the laws of God." His having many wives, was not a secret. Although his plural marriages were with the consent of his female brides, polygamy appeared less muddy than the other charges and may have held up in court. However, polygamy charges may not have been enough to disband the Branch group, although it may have carried heavy penalties.

The contention that Branch believers committed suicide is another area attacked by those questioning the methods of the Federal raid. Bob Ricks, FBI spokesperson, said after the fire, "We went through the world and interviewed former cult members, associates of cult members, the number that I last checked was 61 people. The vast bulk, the substantial majority of those believed that they would not commit suicide." (7)

Investigators, after the inferno on April 19, 1993, found skulls with bullet holes. The circumstances and time of the wounds was never determined. Some suggested that they may have been killed in the raid of February 28, or they could have been a few who committed suicide.

The sum of the matter is that the evidence fog leads many to think that the Government was responsible for the death of Branch believers. It may be a precursor of what will befall future detractors and dissidents. Another manifestation of big government's iron grip squeezing our constitutional freedoms and rights.

Others are not willingly to go as far in their conclusions. They simply blame the Government for exercising poor judgment, for misunderstanding cult-mentality. McLennan County Sheriff Jack Harwell was a 30-year veteran of the area's police force. He was familiar with Branch Davidians, and was present during the 1987 shoot-out between Koresh and Roden. He believed that the ATF had a good plan with the element of surprise. He had cautioned Federal agents against over aggressiveness—bulldozing outbuildings and automobiles and bombardment with loud music and spotlights. (8) He pointed out that the Branch group believed their farm was a sovereign nation. "They were peaceful and normal until you crossed the line uninvited, and then you were an invader", said Harwell. "Error No. 1 was not canceling the raid when they knew for certain it had been blown. . .someone in authority said 'go ahead' and people died." (8)

During the nearly two month siege, Harwell exhorted ATF and FBI teams to pull back during negotiations. "Those folks are trained to deal with hostage rescues", he tells <u>US News and World Report</u>, "Their playbook says you apply unrelenting pressure until they crack.

But the Davidians weren't hostages; they were there by choice. I urged that the agents pull back and give those people room to think and make a better choice, for themselves and for those children. . .When you create elite forces and train and equip them for maximum violence, they want to do what they've been trained to do. When you apply pressure to people with deeply held religious beliefs, all you do is strengthen their resolve." (8)

On the other end of the spectrum, others contended that no matter what the government did, intentionally or from ignorance, they squarely imputed responsibility to the followers of the proclaimed messiah. They allowed themselves to be duped, endangered their lives and the lives of their children. Obviously Branch followers really believed that Vernon Howell was heaven's guide. Koresh had convinced himself that he was "The Lamb of God". In fact, as Sheriff's Harwell suggested, the initial raid may have strengthened their resolve—since they were expecting an attack from the government, this obviously confirmed their beliefs and clinched their faith in Koresh.

That's why many religionists and commentators place the blame on the idea of millennialism, apocalypticism. The former depicts a period (sometimes 1,000 years) of great happiness or perfection—a paragon and consummation of the best hopes of mankind. The latter envisages a time of foreboding and futuristic cataclysms. In their reasoning, these concepts were the hens that hatched the eggs of cultism—the spire that led men up and out of reality to cloudy mansions of utopia. Ultimately, they discover they neither have wings to fly nor promenade on which to travel, and they plunge into terrestrial reality.

An editorial in America magazine put it this way: "Given the rootless heterogeneity of our culture—and a high degree of occupational and geographic mobility—new religious movements have always provided Americans the preferred way of redefining their identities in uncertain times of change. The pathological futurology of a David Koresh reminds us of the risks involved—that religion, especially in the form of radical withdrawal from society, is a thing no less dangerous than splitting the atom. . . .Historically, apocalypticism has been the protest literature of out-groups. It thrives when stable cultural systems are undergoing breakdown and provides, by its characteristic separation from wider culture, a way of getting outside the reigning structure..." (9)

Nonetheless, as even admitted by the editorial, both millennialism and apocalypticism have been forces for growth and great good. "In short," says America magazine, "try imagining early Christianity (a 'sect' or 'cult' within Judaism then) without the urgency of the second coming, the Pilgrim Fathers without their millennial dream, or the abolitionists and even early feminists like Susan B. Anthony and Elizabeth Cady Stanton without the revivalist Great Awakening of the 1830's and 40's. As Frances Fitzgerald put it, that religious revival 'gave rise to every major reform movement of the 19th century.'" (9)

Victor Houteff made these interesting comments about the role of religion: "Now let us see what benefits the kingdoms and nations reaped from coming in contact with the church. Babylon, Medo-Persia, Grecia, and Rome, who came in contact with the church, make up the civilized world of today." (10) He then compares those nations that were, isolated from the church.

"The people who were fortunate enough to be the closest to the religion of Christ," continues Houteff, "are, you will find, the most intelligent, the most prosperous. England, for example, who translated the Bible and published and scattered It throughout the world to all peoples and languages, became the greatest of the nations in its time. Then the United States. . .who less than two centuries ago founded its government upon the principles of the Bible and inscribed on its dollar, IN GOD WE TRUST, and who also established the American Bible Societies, in but a comparatively few years became the greatest of nations.. . .The world was founded upon religion, and you can rest assured that when religion disappears from the earth, the world will disappear with it." (10)

So, where is the solution to be found? We cannot obliterate religion. It is an impossibility. We would eradicate the very thing that has been the dynamo for change and growth since the dawn of time and essentially slice our jugular. We could never control faith by civil means. Such action would not only perpetuate it, it would create the very thing we are trying to avoid—radicalism, insurgency, and fanaticism. Civil agencies are impotent against fanaticism. Resistance often fans the coals, and harassment fuels it. Government attempts to oppress faith or religion, may appear to work at the onset. In the beginning, fear may cause the vulnerable and irresolute to flounder and yield. It will in the end create only more distrust and hatred of government. Waco is a prime example; history speaks even louder.

Force, be it propaganda or arms, or both, may seemingly persuade the majority but in the end the very thing it endeavored to destroy either becomes its very demise or survives to supersede it. Imperial Rome tried to destroy early Christianity through centuries of morbid persecution, only in the end to embrace it to save its crumbling empire. Popery tried desperately to destroy the Protestant Reformation. Instead, Protestantism prospered and, in many ways, became the root that allowed western society to grow into an enormous tree of western culture, a culture that leads the world today.

Some cult-busters and anti-cult personages—from theologians to government officials—think the solution is to define a cult, to outlaw, and to proscribe it. History tells us that that flies in the face of wisdom. You cannot fight ideology with tyranny or oppression. Consider for instance, the subject of cults. That is, cult in its fatalistic sense—real cultism. What is a cult? Is it what you and I determine it to be with all our biases and prejudices? Any group differing from us radically in ideology could be dubbed a cult. What poscribes a cult to one proscribes authentic religion to another. Judaism was viewed with contempt by one nation or another throughout antiquity. Yet, today, it is an accepted religion in much of the world. Christianity was considered a cult by Judaism and by Imperial Rome. Yet, today, western society is professedly Christian. Protestants, during the Middle Ages, were regarded as heretical and faced the pain of death. Much of what is considered acceptable today, whether it be religion or not, was cultic or radical in yesteryear. Seventh-day Adventists, until recently, were considered a cult. It is now one of the fastest growing Christian denominations.

Who can rightly decide what constitutes a cult? The dictionary defines a cult as: "Worship or religious devotion; especially a form of religion. A system of religious observances. Extravagant devotion to a person, cause, or thing; also the object of such devotion." (11) This could describe any religion, and some secular entities as well, radical or not.

Some believe that a cultist is one who has a strong belief in the Bible and the Second Coming of Christ; who home schools his children; who has accumulated survival foods and has a strong belief in the second amendment. This labels nearly all fundamentalist Christians, over 300 different Christian denominations in America, a mountain of militant groups, and hordes of home-schoolers.

If either the church or the state forcefully crushed, what they termed dissident groups, fringe organizations and the like—so-called cults—what would result? History answers. It could become modern-day crusades and inquisitions—the rack, the stake, and executions.

The first and natural reaction to such a thought is repudiation. But, is it really impossible? Is it so outlandish? It is easy to deny this could ever happen in America. Yet, history has demonstrated the opposite, over and over again. One small step leads to another. Civil agencies cannot successfully regulate or repress ideology—dogmas, morality, faith—religion. Civil statutes define crime, and deal with malfeasance and incivility, but it is powerless to regulate morality, matters of conscience, or faith. It cannot teach or punish ideology, morality, or religion. That rests with the individual. For the state to try and control matters of belief could lead to more Wacos. You cannot fight faith with guns. Bullets may kill the body but not the soul of a true religionist. Bars may imprison the mortal frame but not the human spirit. Legistlators may enact laws, but they mean nothing if they contradict a genuine believers faith. They answer to a higher law. Any form of repression would only drive adherents deeper into the very thing from which we would try to extricate them. In trying to pluck them from deception, we may unwittingly, push them over the very precipice from which we seek their rescue. This may be precisely what happened with the Branch group. We cannot be sure, but who can honestly say that it was not a part of the tragedy?

Faith is an enigma of man. It is something that happens deep within the human spirit. Resolve within the devout strengthens with any form of oppression. One's right to believe is as valid as one's right to live. We must agree with Alonzo Jones, commentator on religion and government, who wrote, "A man who surrenders his right to believe surrenders God. Consequently, no man, no association or organization of men, can ever rightly ask of any man a surrender of his right to believe. Every man has the right, so far as organizations of men are concerned, to believe as he pleases; and that right, so long as he is a Protestant, so long as he is a Christian, yes, so long as he is a man, he never can surrender, and he never will." (12) For a man to surrender his right to believe is to surrender his "right to think". (14) Any move by the state perceived as an attack on this right, has produced villains, heroes, traitors, and martyrs.

Polygamy, sex with minors, adultery, and murder are not acceptable behaviors. It stands in violation of civil laws and is a breach of moral rectitude. Most would concede to this no matter their religious persuasion. Branch Davidians claimed to be Christian. Yet, most Christians would agree that the Bible flatly condemns their actions. Their use of guns also comes into question. "Whosoever shall smite thee on thy right cheek," says Jesus, turn thee to the other also." (13) John, author of the book of Revelation, a book Koresh used extensively, wrote: "He that killeth with the sword must be killed with the sword"(14) Conservative, devout Christians would no doubt point out that the Christian's weapons are love, hope, and faith. Branch Davidians may have evaded definitive proof of their guilt in the eyes of the law, but they did not evade the eyes of virtuosity or standard Christian practice.

How do we prevent another David Koresh? Should we allow any group to do as they please in the name of religion? The only way to effectively combat the problem is to appeal to the mind, to reason, the very thing exercised to create faith. It is nigh impossible to reason with a Vernon Howell turned David Koresh. We may never alter self-proclaimed messiahs or deified apostles. We cannot quench the thirst for power, or the appetite for veneration. Thorough, honest education will ax the tree of fanaticism and keep it a virtual stump. The alternative, civil and religious aggression, leads to bloodshed, anger, distrust, and perpetual revolution. Education will preserve the rights and the dignity of man—pillars of the Constitution. It unravels the tightly knit fabric of genuine cultism.

 The spirit of tolerance is the engine of freedom and progress. The spirit of intolerance is the generator of tyranny. Tolerance requires patience and hard work. It preserves the body and soul of individuality and nationality. Intolerance self-destructs. It may not happen immediately, but eventually it will happen. Search history and see!

 Again, the lethal weapon is education's appeal to reason. Educate at all levels of society. Several keys, to both the secular and the religious world, can bolt the bars on cultism. First, we must teach men and women in society, in the churches, in the synagogues, in the mosques, and in the temples, to think and reason—clearly and honestly—for themselves. Second, teach society to pursue truth at all cost. Third, never, never, surrender your judgment to another, no matter his experience, station, education, or charisma. Fourth, exemplify the courage to preserve these principles. If we are to prevent another Waco, we must aim to educate on every level to make these four elements our arrowhead. A tall order but doable.

 The ability to reason for oneself is one of life's most precious commodities. Much of mankind is content to be led—content to let others reason for them—content to go along for the ride and let others navigate the way. We depend upon experts to work it out and then tell us. Our educational system teaches us to pattern and copy. Often it does not teach us to reason from cause to effect, to freethink, to conscientiously act upon our own conclusions. Sheepish human-kind tends to follow the crowd, to fear ostracism for being different. A society or organization of free-thinkers, of citizens or constituents who can reason. Who are encouraged to make decisions based upon their own research. Who are allowed to follow their own convictions will develop giant intellects and trendsetters, persons not easily swayed by cheap and inconsistent rhetoric. Having learned critical thinking, such persons will find it hard to surrender their discretion to another.

The second principle encourages an earnest reverence for truth. We are bombarded with information from the media, from religious leaders, from friends, and sometimes from our families, which we inhale as pure air. If you have ever traveled to a foreign country and have read or listened to the news, you may have been surprised to hear a different side of the same report you had heard at home. Interviews are often reported far differently than originally related Books tell the same stories from varying perspectives. The same story with the same facts can be made to portray conflicting messages. It is only natural, and beneficial, that subjects be viewed in various ways. Nearly everything is told by mankind from his own national, personal, or religious bent, rarely without bias. Sometimes deliberately. Sometimes not. Whether deliberate or otherwise, propaganda exists everywhere. An uncompromising pursuit of truth, an insistence to know all sides before judgment, will create a more honest society, a more effective church. People will tolerate less duplicity. Citizens and parishioners will not easily accept reports without thorough and objective thought. Sensationalism, traditionalism, preconceptions, prejudices, and appearances, will not find easy targets in these individuals. A well-informed populace is one of the best prevention of corruption and vice .

Closely related to independent thinking is independent judgment. One should never surrender judgment or reason to another— no matter his claim, his devotion, his uprightness, or his appearance. One author wrote: the mind who surrenders his judgment completely to another will sooner or later be deceived. (15) Both secular and church entities ignore this salient point. It happens throughout society, but no where is it more pervasive than in religion. We trust and respect our clergy, our spiritual leaders, and rightly we should. None the less, no prelate should be allowed to steal our right to independent judgment. Whether done wittingly or unwittingly, church leaders condition parishioners to look to them as the unquestioned authority. Guides they must be, unquestioned authority they cannot be. The voice of the prelate, must be the voice leading men to the inviolable standards. He, too, must be subject to the very standards that gave him authority to lead in the first place.

Using the comparison of the civil realm, a church leader is neither a legislator, a judge, nor a policeman. He is an instructor of the law. He may encourage, admonish, educate, persuade citizens to uphold civil injunctions. He can neither make nor enforce the law. A minister's power resides in suasion. He convinces by reason, based upon the authority and the foundation of his faith. For Jews and Christians, this authority is the Bible. He must exemplify in actions the "law" he claims to defend. A leader of parishioners guides constituents in understanding and in honoring core principles - the basis of their faith. They are not to become creators of faith and objects of veneration. They are not to take advantage of their parishioners' conscience. Parishioners are co-workers not ideological slaves. When you have one or few individuals determining the fate of the community, you have cultism. Any organization that dishonors and disrespects the free-will of its membership, that tries to manipulate their consciences, be it ever so subtle, is deadly.

Mankind can never reliably guide without checks and balances. We have too great a capacity for self-deception—contrary to humanist's thinking. History supports this. One writer said: "As long as you ask the question you think that should be answered for you, without taking heed of my assurance that you are in greater need of certain other instruction—so long will I be unable to help you and so long will you believe that I am no use to you. One maxim of the Near East says:

"But you, in ignorance of the instruction which you need, will inevitably conclude that there is some other reason for our not being in concert and harmony. You invent the reason—and your self-esteem makes it 'true' for you". (16)

True spiritual guides will not become laws unto themselves, consistently impugning and injuring evident reasoning. They will not view questions on teachings, from parishioners, as a threat. They will not suppress one's right to think or to differ. They will not draw attention primarily to themselves. A governing body, or conference—receptor of your affections, finances, and hopes—professing the fundamentals of the faith but practicing them only when convenient, will sooner or later deceive you. In spite of good intentions, past good works and aspirations, the mind that yields itself unabridged to another will fall victim to delusion.

Religion, today, is riddled with subtle cultism. While clinging to the creeds of their fathers, they attempt amending their religion to suit their modern leaders' inclinations. This happens imperceptibly at first, because most laity do not study for themselves but quickly embrace their teachers' explanations. Such leaders slowly draw the masses to themselves, and become the guardians of the faith. Constituents find themselves tempted to idolize their apparently devout leaders. Convinced of their sincerity, the laity almost unconsciously surrender their minds, their reason, their power. Independent judgment is sold to the genius and station of faulty, spiritual guides. Why? We trust our ministers. We develop immoderate confidence in them and accept their decisions almost without question. Contented we let them pilot our faith. This subtle cultism is extremely perilous.

Consider, for example, ministers who tell their members not to listen to certain persons differing in theology, or to trash periodicals differing from traditional thinking. Some Pastors have encouraged their flock to stop speaking to members holding divergent opinions. This behavior quickly places the hierarchy on the defensive. Can the church afford this spirit of intolerance? No! Sooner or later, it will reap the fruit of its own planting. Cultism benefits the one or the few, not the many. It limits the masses to the leader is thinking and no higher. Real cultism, therefore, is the enslaving of reasoning and diligent free-thinking, the stagnation of knowledge. The Middle Ages is both witness and example.

Cultism is not only a stumbling block for religionists, but it is a stumbling block for all humanity. If this appears exaggerated, consider that most of us accept something one way, and find it hard to change and accept it another way. Confidence in methodology, and the standard leadership, whether in the medical profession; or the educational system, makes the status quo nigh impossible to rear-range. We readily promote findings and guidance of our leaders and accept their methodology as norms. Do we normally stop to con-sider how other countries operate in these specific areas? Do we assess our beliefs, whether they be secular or religious? Do we listen to others who may differ from the norm? Those who do not practice traditional methods of healing are often termed quacks. Although they could be just as knowledgeable as college graduates in a spe-cific area, those who do not hold decrees are not considered experts. This is not a condemnation of our medical or educational system. It is an illustration, using two very important areas of western society.

Its simply not easy for us to change, to accept new belief systems. Many belong to a particular faith because they were either born in it or brought up in it from an early age. To many going to church is not a conscientious matter, but tradition. They have devel-oped confidence in their leaders, and their church. It becomes diffi-cult to change their faith. They become followers, surrendering their religious mind and devotion to the church.

Subtle cultism becomes overt in the hands of charismatic, bold leaders, claiming homage in most or all matters of their parishio-ners' lives. Such prelates metamorphose from mere mortals to gods. Personal choices, family ties, and finances, are surrendered to these teachers who become the light instead of the lamp, the water instead of the faucet. When the populous discovers that they are mere mor-tals, it is often too late. By then, they have been swept into a whirl-pool of devotion and loyalty.

The above has been perfectly demonstrated in numerous groups, Branch Davidians being only one of them. It has become prominent when speaking of cults. So, we should examine the Branch group in light of what we have discussed.

When Benjamin Roden separated, in 1955, from the Davidian Association, he capitalized on disappointment surrounding Houteff's death. Without Houteff, believers looked for someone else to lead them. Roden grabbed the opportunity. He craved a following and power. To harvest that power, he needed an instrument, a message—something new, something different. The "Branch" was born. To pave the way for the new doctrines, which would otherwise easily be recognized as contrary to fundamental beliefs, he developed a concept known as "the living Spirit of Prophecy." Although, originally conceived by Houteff, Roden added new meaning. Its important for us to review this idea as it played a key role in the eventual development of David Koresh.

Houteff taught that God has and will continue to send messages to man. Such messages will come through human agents, but that the man was just a vessel, an instrument in conveying these truths. That in every age God sent a message to direct his people, in this sense the Word of God is ever living. "The ever-unfolding", says Houteff, "Inspired interpretations of the Scriptures is the ever-living Spirit of Prophecy" (17) "The Spirit of Prophecy, therefore, is God's means of communicating from Heaven directly to His church on earth, as well as of unfolding the sealed prophecies to her." (17) As a Christian, he also pointed out that the Bible is to be the sure test by which any parishioner may know whether or not the claimant-prophet was authentic. Conservative Davidian SDAs still hold this view.

Roden, on the other hand, taught that you must have a living individual at all times to guide the church. This mandated the physical presence of a prophet to direct the laity at all times. Thus, members were conditioned to look more upon the human agent than the message. Therefore, Roden, a charismatic leader intrinsically gained the confidence of members although his message contradicted established and obvious biblical thought. They soon surrendered their judgment to Roden, ignoring all contradictions. This action led souls further and further out to sea into the foggy mist of fate, a fate that rested in the hands of a man seeking self-exaltation.

By 1986, the Branch's ship was already desultorily adrift. Three Branch members, after the death of Lois Roden, told the author that they were looking for another prophet to come and lead them. They were shown that much of the Branch teachings were contrary to clear biblical teaching, contrary to the foundation of their faith. Puzzled, bewildered, and sometimes dumbfounded, they kept repeating that they must have someone to lead them.

One did come, Vernon Howell, who eventually became David Koresh and led Branch believers into the flames. These congenial, well-meaning, and kind ladies surrendered their reasoning and judgment to another. They were content to have another direct their convictions. To those seeking self-aggrandizement, such members provided a field of dreams. However, in the end, it became a mirage, a quick sand of tragedy.

The notion of needing a living human agent, at all times, to guide and to interpret the bible has been the gin for numerous Davidian believers. It has created many splinters. As one individual claims the prophetic office, another soon arises to do the same, then a third, all with varying views and solutions. All have one thing in common, a leadership practically worshipped by its followers. A situation not unique to Davidia but common to numerous groups.

Such leaders do not always start out by declaring the prophetic office. They often start with new concepts which covertly point to themselves. Gradually the direction shifts homage to them. Lives of their followers are controlled directly or in directly by their teacher. Constituents think they serve God, but in reality they serve the so-called messenger, as testified to by those who have escaped different groups.

In one group, the Davidian leader claims, like David Koresh, to be the modern day "King David." Members pray and baptize in his name. He too, claims the right to many wives, and has commanding control over his followers.

Can another Waco happen? Yes, if we do not understand or combat the phenomenon of cultism with honest reasoning and conscientious action. Branchites were not the only group suffering from cultism. In almost every walk of life, men and women place undue confidence into the hands of their leaders. Whether subtle or overt, our minds are being programmed to subliminally surrender our greatest weapons, our reason and judgment. We must, as a society, as a church, determine not to accept information at face value, but to persevere, to objectively study, to research for ourselves, to vigorously pursue truth no matter the cost. We must be willing to stand for the right at the expense of even our lives. We can then live as free men, having neither the chains of oppression, the bands of anarchy, nor the weight of ideological slavery—cultism.

Chapter 10

Let The Whole World Know

"Our faith shall not fail us,and our hope shall not be in vain, for God has not forsaken the earth. He Who rules and guides the stars in their unerring path, is able to lead us safely to our own land." (1) These words, spoken by Victor Houteff in a 1947 sermon, may best express the spirit of the fundamentalist Davidian movement. It has been conspicuously and severely bruised by fate. Yet, Davidia believes their faith shall not fail them. Their hopes in the establishment of a kingdom of peace amidst the greatest distress to face mankind will not be in vain. One day the world will come to know by sight what they know by faith. The Davidian Seventh-day Adventists community endured international scrutiny during the 1993 siege. Yet their hopes, their aspirations, their faith and their courage went unnoticed.

The thrusting of Branch Davidians onto the world stage inadvertently brought all of Adventism into scrutiny. The microscope, however, focused on Davidia. Officials and the media quickly foraged through years past and found what, on the surface, appeared to be another scion of radicalism—a group on the fringe.

The SDA denomination, although profoundly affected, found it easier to smother the blaze of negative publicity. It pointed to a several- million-world-membership, hospitals, colleges and universities as a kind of acceptance card. The public found it more difficult to push them outside the mainstream.

Davidia had little to shield them from the world's steely gaze. Davidia was an outcast of the denomination. It was neither wealthy nor large, and by the time of the shoot-out in 1993, had already experienced brutal disappointments, and divisions. The movement had been ridiculed by its opponents, misrepresented by its friends, betrayed by self-seekers, and well-nigh choked by fanatics. It appeared that Davidia was just another group of deluded enthusiasts about to self-destruct. They were easy to blackball—conspicuous targets for the mainstream. For most, just hearing the word cult, was sufficient evidence to skewer them. They were guilty of extremism if nothing else. It was easy to publish misinformation. Who cared? Who would successfully challenge established thought? Davidian SDAs were too dissimilar, too unconventional to be propitious. In Davidia, the establishment saw something to dread. Prejudice and trepidation had always been Davidia's greatest opponents. Accustomed to facing this two-headed beast within their denomination, they were shocked to meet its spiny claws and penetrating bite from those outside Adventism. The February 28, shoot-out, which killed four federal agents, seemed to sever public sympathy and to seal Davidia's lot. Whether an orthodox believer or a Branch member, it did not matter, the name Davidian Seventh-day Adventists had suffered irreparable damage.

This dim view of events, surrounding the Branch fiasco, has not deterred faith or progress of orthodox members. Although some left the movement, and others went underground or became disillusioned, fundamentalists clung to hope. In short, since the death of Victor Houteff and the subsequent "knock-out blow," Davidia was like a broken piece of pottery, shattered by one mishap after another. But the movement bears its water still. It offers its church, although in a damaged earthen vessel, libation of which, they are certain, is the message of Heaven. Not only to the SDA denomination, but they believe that one day the world will taste of this life-giving beverage. Davidia believes God has sent a special message to mankind to direct our steps in these days of peril. It is only a matter of time before it is all brought to light along with a people who will truly represent the character of Heaven. This is what they want the world to know.

They admit that generally they have failed to appropriately represent the message. Yet, of one thing they are certain, the series of studies, brought to light from the Scriptures by Houteff, are not cunning fabrications of human reasoning. But are God's words for mankind at the eleventh-hour of earth's history. Truly committed, orthodox believers are not daunted by disappointment, bad publicity, misrepresentation, or self-servers. Since the death of the movement's founder, they have had plenty of opportunities to hone their faith.

The stupor brought on by the 1950's and 1960's "knock-out

blow", opened the way for a grab-bag—a prophet here, a prophet there. Members, not completely disenchanted, found their way to one or another. For years, orthodox believers were ravaged by gales of immoderate new doctrines. No sooner could one group form, before another would step forward proclaiming some new idea. What one approved another condemned. By the 1980's, a large part of Davidia was trapped in a whirlwind of schisms. It may have appeared, to an outsider, that at any time Davidia would be swept into oblivion.

Examples of this phenomenon range across educational backgrounds, status, and nationalities, from the ridiculous to the absurd. Michael (an assumed name), a gifted, orthodox Davidian Bible teacher, walked quickly along a New York City sidewalk on a sunny day in 1986. It wasn't long before he discovered a tall, well-dressed, middle aged man, enthusiastically distributing literature. (2) It was not the first time Michael had observed someone canvassing, but this man appeared different. After a brief discussion, Michael asked, "Are you a Seventh-day Adventist?" "Yes", John (an assumed name) cheerfully replied. The conversation progressed. Sensing his sincerity, Michael continued, "What you're giving out is good"... but... did you know that there is more?...more light". Having sparked his interest, Michael arranged a Bible study with the zealous church member. Within days John was thrilled with his newly found knowledge and eagerly soaked up the new teachings. His fervor reached new heights when he began traveling with Michael and other teachers. (2)

Within weeks, to everyone's consternation, John suddenly claimed divine enlightenment and later launched his own movement. A year or so later he announced that God's judgments would begin in April, 1988. (2) John has since disappeared from view.

M.T. Jordan was a West Indian émigré living in Canada. In early 1982, he was a Davidian teacher and member of M.J. Bingham's Bashan group. He was disciplined by Bingham for reportedly vying for power—which posed a threat to Bingham who, himself, claimed to be a prophet. (2) During a visit to Trinidad, his country of birth, Jordan conversed with Elton (an assumed name), a Davidian friend, who claimed heavenly inspiration. But Elton apparently lacked enough charisma to command a sizable following. He, reportedly, changed his doctrines like a fashion model changes garments. Elton privately shared his newest insights with Jordan. Within months of his return to Canada, Jordan proclaimed that he was the recipient of new light. Although that light was not new to Elton, it was god-sent to the unwary and to many of Bingham's followers. (2)

Jordan did not look back. His following grew rapidly. By 1985, He became prophet and president of a group larger than the Branch. Like Roden he drastically altered the original message. Like Koresh he eventually proclaimed himself modern-day King David, had body guards, and had established his own "House of David," including a harem. Devoted adherents prayed in his name and surrendered sizable portions of their earthly goods to the man they referred to as "king". The group has dwindled, but still operates. (2)

The man who coronated Jordan as king, later, declared his own call to the prophetic office. He formulated another group, but, after some years of operation, disbanded.

These examples are typical of the fanatical workings of Davidia from the close of Old Mt. Carmel Center to the 1990's. "It seems like Davidia manufactures prophets!" is the sentiment of some Davidians. As one scans the landscape, it appears that Davidia has been convulsed by a storm of doctrines. As disquieting as this was, particularly to traditional believers, it was not altogether discouraging to the faithful. It certainly would not have been a surprise to Houteff had he lived. Remember, he foretold of this unfortunate state of affairs. But he also spoke of Davidia's eventual triumph. Thus, dedicated believers declare that this is all temporary—Victory is assured in due time, in spite of circumstances.

The fundamental, Davidian community, although much embarrassed by fanatical elements, was not free of problems among themselves. Minute doctrinal differences, mismanagement, and power struggles, among some would-be leaders, riddled their ranks. It was an unsettling, perpetual trial. As a result, some individuals faded into the background. Others started their own, personal ministries. Some

Some disassociated themselves and became bitter. Amazingly, three or four groups emerged, became viable organizations, developed contacts throughout the US, Canada, and several foreign countries and are still growing.

Other than the Waco disaster, the waters in the 1990's thus far are relatively calm, except for an occasional ripple. This has come about, as one by one, fanatical elements fizzed to a bubble, here or there. As a result, orthodoxers' numbers increase as more and more Adventists come into contact with the original message. This later success is owed, in part, to free-thinkers. Uninhibited by prejudice and tradition, they find it easier to brave brash opposition of denominational leaders. They respond to the swell of information distributed throughout the denomination which allows members to study unbiasedly for themselves. Furthermore, there is a growing lack of trust for denominational leadership. The world Church's growing intolerance for other doctrinal views, and those who would question its authority. Its growing liberalism, disposing of formerly accepted standards, and, what is generally perceived as lack of substantial edification from the pulpit, has led braver sorts to investigate other ideas within the fundamental framework of Adventism. With the growth of true Davidians, exhibiting a much more representative deportment in harmony with the original message, Davidian SDAs are reaching their reluctant counterparts. It has not yet returned to its former glory, but it is making headway.

Today, there are at least three primary orthodox groups, and a few smaller ones. There are one or two larger groups like those mentioned earlier, who, like Ben Roden, deviated from the fundamentals and have become cultic, but they are declining, and fundamentalism is growing.

No one really knows the precise number of believers. It could be as high as 25,000 students with a few thousand hard-core believers world-wide. They make up the constituents of several groups, and many are closet believers. It is known, according to one record, that there were nearly five thousand students in Africa in 1987 and 1988. There are cases where whole churches embraced "The

Shepherd's Rod." Some are unaware of organized groups, but carry out their convictions living and teaching its precepts and doctrines, sometimes partially, and sometimes in full. Some are leaders in their local churches, unbeknown to the denominational officials. Their additional faith known to just a few.

Discovering unknown members can be illustrated by numerous incidents. One that stands out took place in the Netherlands during a World General Conference of SDAs. While Davidian workers distributed literature and conducted discussions with attendees, a man from India approached one of the workers and asked, "What is the name of this message?...What is it?...I want to know precisely. .." He gently insisted on an answer. "This is the Shepherd's Rod", replied the worker, who expected a verbal tirade or scorching denunciation. Instead, the questioner jubilantly called his father who was a short distance away. "I told you!...I told you!...This was the same message that grandfather taught us...I knew it!...I knew it!" Apparently his grandfather was a Rod-believer in India and died believing the Davidian message, but not before teaching it to his posterity.

We know there are Davidian SDAs in Europe, Africa, Asia, The South Seas, The West Indies, Central and South America, and of course in the US and Canada. Since the denomination comprises over eight million members, Davidians have not fully impacted the church or reached the level of contacts of the 1940's and 50's the movement's zenith. Nonetheless, it is reviving from its nearly fatal blow in the 1960's, slowly climbing out of its quicksand of stupefaction. The fact that it has survived is, by anyone's standard, a miracle. The fact that it is growing and showing signs of recovery, is amazing, and indicates that Davidia will not disappear from the world's landscape.

A complete recovery of Davidia is not entirely impossible. It may be a formidable task. It will require more miracles, more providential intervention. They have already survived stupendous odds—60 years of vilification, misrepresentation, persecution of all sorts. They have survived years of battling fanaticism, indifference, and impropriety from within their own ranks. One small but positive miracle occurred in 1986 when two influential groups conducted an unprecedented transaction, they merged.

It is easy to dismiss the Davidian view of things as typical, religious, behavioral response. It may be tempting to think that it is the natural tendency of humanity to hold on to a cherished cause in spite of disillusionment and defeat. Sociologist may quickly dub it another enigma of mankind, or patronize it as the dynamics of religious orders. Before giving way to cynicism, there are several things to consider—matters that make the Davidian situation unique. Maybe no sociological model adequately fit it.

The reasons are actually not too difficult to understand. Perhaps the most outstanding reason is the Davidian message—the very heart and soul of the movement. As we have already seen, "The Shepherd's Rod" teachings, or the Davidian message, is in itself unique. It is revolutionary, not in the sense of violence as portrayed by the Branch which was not a representation of it at all. It is revolutionary, because it is so different from the message of any other Christian company. It is not at all dissimilar to its counterpart—the teachings of Adventism, because it is both in accord with and based upon biblical Adventism. It is not a mass of disjointed dogmas and ideas. Whether you agree or disagree, it follows a biblical continuity, captivating on one hand and challenging on the other.

This is especially true when viewing current events. Victor Houteff's exposition of Scripture, written over 50 years ago, beside the specific events to take place in the SDA denomination, forecasted a future world war in the Middle East, that Communism, unfortunately, would resurge and gain a strong political role in the up-coming cataclysms that is to engulf western society—cataclysms that is to include an unprecedented world economic crisis, the collapse of the western world, The State of Israel and the Islamic community. In the midst of these woes, according to Davidian teachings, God will establish his long awaited biblical kingdom of Glory promised to ancient King David. It will offer an unquestionable demonstration of all the good God intended for mankind from the beginning.

The prospect of the Davidic kingdom may appear far from

shore, or preposterous to common thinking. However, whether we care to admit it or not, a careful study of international developments reveals that the other events may not be impossible of reaching harbor. Although it may seem unlikely now, some authorities on economics and world affairs see the possibility of a world market collapse, and a Communist rise. Given this scenario, it is possible to experience the fall of the United Nations, the devastation of Israel and the Arab world. Of course, time will tell all.

The Davidian or "Rod" message forecasts these events by showing that the Ancient biblical seers wrote parallel to their time, backdrop, and circumstances typifying our time and circumstances. In this setting of typology, Bablylon, Assyria, Rome, all have parallels to some aspect of our modern world, and their demise prognosticates our own. Its built-in, Davidians believe. Its inevitable because human nature is the same and God saw it all in advance and he controls the results. The strengths and weaknesses of Ancient Israel, their victories and failures, faithfulness and unfaithfulness, are all chronicles in type and antitype. History and prophecy are etched in fate's stony book all at once. This principle of Davidian ideology can be mind-boggling when seen in actual text application. If not it is certainly challenging; more so when every portion of Davidic doctrine seems to remarkably harmonize with itself throughout its numerous theological pieces. This uncanny phenomenon is admitted even by its skeptics.

It is this that makes Davidia unique among unpopular sects, especially with current events as they are. The strong possibility of Victor Houteff being right will not leave the Davidian adherent, or cease to haunt the once convicted follower. Not until time and fate irrefutably erase all hope will Davidians completely fade away with yesterday. Tomorrow will either find Davidians looming before us as guides through future's stormy seas or shipwrecked on the shores of misadventure. Obviously the time for either has not yet come. Scrapes and near misses in the past has not yet stopped it from sailing. Embarrassed, disappointed, shaken, and disoriented, somehow it maneuvers its way through straits and violent waves. So, we are destined to meet Davidia again. Perhaps you may meet again, for a while, another radical Davidian band having left the fundamentals and who may bring more embarrassment. But they will not be the real Davidians. One day you may meet them—the genuine. This time, it will not be with oozies, hand grenades, or strapnels—a one man show, beer-drinking, rock music, or polygamy. They will not have firearms. They will possess the most powerful weapon of all, faith—a conviction in something they believe to be right—the soul grip of biblical themes fastened so tightly that their hearts and minds are constrained.

If words would escape them, they would borrow the declaration of the eloquent New Testament Writer, Paul of Tarsus, who wrote: "For God, who commanded the light to shine out of darkness, hath shined in our hearts. . . We are troubled on every side, yet not distressed; we are perplexed, but not in despair; persecuted, but not forsaken; cast down, but not destroyed." (3) This is what you should know about Davidian Seventh-day Adventists.

THE END.

Notes to Chapter 1

1. Testimonials of pioneers, friends, former believers, and observers.
2. VT Houteff, "Timely Greetings," Universal Publishing Assn., vol. 2 #28 pp. 15-18.
3. Letter from the Executive Council, Oct. 13, 1995, pp. 1-4.
4. "Obituary of Benjamin Roden," Waco Tribune-Herald, Oct. 30, 1978.
5. George Roden, (to the editor), Waco Tribune-Herald, Dec. 13, 1978.
6. Ray Bell, "Dispute Between Davidian Sects Reaches Waco Court," Waco Tribune-Herald, Nov. 4, 1965.
7. "Testimony Begins in Land Suit Between Davidian Sects," Waco Tribune-Herald, Nov. 5, 1965.
8. Ray Bell, "Smoldering Dispute Flares," Dallas Morning News, Nov. 15, 1987.
9. Allan Nelson, "Religious Sect Fights to Keep County Land," Tribune—Herald, Sunday, Oct. 18, 1987.
10 "Timely Greetings," vol. 1 #24 p. 13.
11. VT Houteff, "Tract No. 14," Universal Publishing Assn., p. 22.
12. "Timely Greetings," vol. 1 #5 pp. 16-18.
13. Clifford L. Linedecker, "Massacre at Waco, Texas," St. Martin's Paperback, 1993, p. 80.
14. Ivan Solotaroff and John Serry, "The Last Revelation from Waco," Esquire Magazine, July 1993, p. 54.
15. See #13.
16. Alan Nelson and Sandra Gines, "Crying in the Wilderness," Tribune Herald, Sunday, Jan. 17, 1988, p. 1A.
17. "The Massacre of the Branch Davidians," Committee for Waco.
18. Drew Parma, "Officers Investigate Rodenville Shooting," Tribune-Herald, Nov. 5, 1987.
19. See #16, p. 8A.
20. "8 Arrested in Connection With Shooting," Tribune-Herald, Nov. 4, 1987.
21. Ray Bell, "Religious Groups' Smoldering Dispute Erupts in Gunfire," Dallas Morning News, Nov. 1987.
22. Tommy Witherspoon, "Rodenville Charges Dismissal to be Sought," Tribune-Herald, Friday, Jan. 22, 1988.
23. See #13, p. 74.
24. Allan Nelson, "Roden Appeal on Mother's Estate Refused," Tribune-Herald, Thursday, Jan, 28, 1988.
25. See #13, pp. 93-94.
26. Ibid, p. 121.

Notes to Chapter 2

1. VT Houteff, "Timely Greetings," Universal Publishing Assn., vol. 1 #18
       p. 22.
2. Testimonials of earlier workers and pioneers.
3. VT Houteff, "Timely Greetings," Universal Publishing Assn., vol. 2 #35
       pp. 23,24.
4. Same as #2.
5. E.G. White, "The Desire of Ages, "Pacific Press Publishing Assn.:
       p.357.
6. Testimonial of an earlier worker.
7. "Timely Greetings," vol. 2 #35 p. 12.
8. Ibid pp. 29, 30.
9. "Timely Greetings," vol. 1 #50 p. 26.
10. Testimonials of earlier workers and friends.
11. VT Houteff, "The Symbolic Code," Universal Publishing Assn. vol. 10 #7
       pp. 9, 10.
12. Exodus 31:18 (KJV).
13. "Timely Greetings," vol. 2 #35 p. 17.
14. Ibid pp. 19, 20.
15. Ibid pp. 21, 22.
16. 1 Corinthians 1:20 (KJV).
17. "Timely Greetings," vol. 2 #35 p. 23.
18. Ibid
19. VT Houteff, "Tract #7" Universal Publishing Assn., p. 6.
20. "Timely Greetings," vol. 1 #27 pp. 7, 8.
21. Psalm 23:3 (KJV).
22. Exodus 4:17 (KJV).
23. "Tract No. 7," pp. 6, 7.
24. Ibid p. 8.
25. Ibid p. 10.
26. Ibid p. 11.
27. Micah 6:9 (KJV).

Notes to Chapter 3

1. James White, "Life Incidences," Steam Press of SDA Publishing Assn., pp.28-33.
2. E.G. White, "The Great Controversy, Pacific Press Publishing Assn. p. 599.
3. Daniel 8:14 (KJV).
4. "Life Incidences," pp. 38, 39.
5. "The Great Controversy," pp. 324, 325.
6. Ibid pp. 330-332.
7. Ibid p. 368.
8. Ibid p. 401.
9. Ezra 7:13-27 (KJV).
10. Daniel 9:25 (KJV).
11. Ibid 8:17-26
12. "Life Incidences," p. 182.
13. "The Great Controversy," p. 343.
14. VT Houteff, "The Answerer," Universal Publishing Assn., Bk. no. Ip. 47.
15. Trustees of Ellen G. White Estate, Historical Prologue of "Early Writings," March, 1963 pp. 18, 19.
16. Delbert Baker, "The Unknown Prophet, Review and Herald Publishing Assn., pp. 21, 29.
17. Ibid p. 61.
18. William Foy, "Christian Experience," p. 23.
19. "The Unknown Prophet," p. 88.
20. Ibid p. 125.
21. J.N. Loughborough, "The Great Second Advent Movement," pp 182, 11
22. E.G. White, "Testimonies for the Church," Pacific Press Publishing Assn., vol. 1 pp. 11-13.
23. E.G. White, "Early Writings, Review and Herald Publishing Assn. pp. 14, 15.
24. Ibid p. 20.
25. Trustees of E.G. White Estate, Historical Prologue of "Early Writings, March 1963, p. 17.
26. "Testimonies for the Church," vol. 1 p. 71.
27. "Seventh-day Adventist Year Book, Review and Herald Publishing Assn..
28. Trustees of E.G. White Estate, pp. 20, 21.
29. "Testimonies for the Church, "vol. 1 p. 76.
30. Ibid p. 75.
31. E.G. White, "A Word to the Little Flock," Review and Herald Publishing Assn., p. 12
32. "The Great Controversy," pp. 429, 430.
33. Ibid pp. 431, 432.
34. 1 Corinthians 3:16, 17 (KJV).

Notes to Chapter 3 continue

35. E.G. White, "The Spirit of Prophecy Treasure Chest," Pacific Press
       Publishing Assn., p. 23.
36. George I. Butler, "Review and Herald "magazine, June 9, 1874.
37. Statement by J.N. Loughborough.
38. E.G. White, "Life Sketches, Pacific Press Publishing Assn. p. 449.
39. E.G. White, "Testimonies to Ministers, Pacific Press Publishing Assn.,
       pp. 79, 80.
40. Ibid p. 468.
41. E.G. White, "Selected Messages," Review and Herald Publishing Assn.,
bk. 1 p. 234, 235.
42. E.G. White, Letter 24, 1892.
43. E.G. White Letter 2A, 1892, pp. 43, 44.
44. 8.6. White to OA Olsen, May 31, 1896.
45. "Testimonies for the Church," vol. 5 p. 217.
46. "Selected Messages," bk. 1 p. 128.
47. The SDA General Conference Bulletin, 34th session, vol. 4 extra April 3,
       1901, p. 25 cols. 1, 2.
48. E.G. White, "Review And Herald," magazine July 24, 1888.
49. Sylvester Bliss, "Memoirs of William Miller, (Boston: Joshua V. Himes.
       1853), pp. 4, 28, 29, 30.

Notes to Chapter 4

1. A.T. Jones, "Civil Government and Religion," American Sentinel, Oakland, CA; New York, NY; Atlanta, GA., p. 21.
2. Matthew 5:44 (KJV)
3. VT Houteff, "The Great Controversy Over 'The Shepherd's Rod,'" Universal Publishing Assn., pp. 51-56 (Tract No. 7)
4. E.G. White, "Counsels to Parents, Teachers and Students," Pacific Press Publishing Assn., p. 86.
5. Agatha Thrash, MD, "Home Remedies," Thrash Publications, p. 5.
6. VT Houteff, "Jezreel Letters," Universal Publishing Assn., #3 p. 12
7. "Jezreel Letters," #9 p. 46.
8. VT Houteff, "Tract No. 1," Universal Publishing Assn., pp. 471, 472.
9. VT Houteff, "The Symbolic Code," Universal Publishing Assn. vol. 1 #7 p.1.
10. VT Houteff, "The Answerer," Universal Publishing Assn.,bk. #3 pp. 62,63.
11. W.G. Wirth letter to W.E. read, February 25, 1955.
12. Church Record Book #3, of clerk of the SDA Church at 54th Street, Los Angeles, CA; Margaret Lane Robb, church clerk, letter to M.E. Kern, dated June 11, 1955.
13. v. I. Houteff, "Timely Greetings," Universal Publishing Assn., vol. 2 #10 pp. 17, 18.
14. "History and Teachings of The Shepherd's Rod," The Committee on Defense Literature of the General Conference of Seventh-day Adventists, October, 1955, p. 6.
15. "Timely Greetings," vol. 2 #26 pp. 21, 22.
16. "Seventh-day Adventist Church Manual," revised 1981, p. 250.7
18. E.G. White, "Testimonies to Ministers," Pacific Press Publishing Assn., pp. 70, 71
19. E.G. White, "Counsels to Writers and Editors," Pacific Press Publishing Assn., p. 27.
20. 1 Thessolonians 5:21 (KJV).
21. "Tract No. 7" p. 34.
22. -"The Great Controversy"-p.- 385.
23. "Tract No. 7," pp. 14, 15.
24. Ibid p. 16.
25. Ibid pp. 19, 20.
26. Ibid p. 21.
27. "History and Teachings of The Shepherd's Rod," p. 13.
28. "Tract No. 7," pp. 14, 15.
29. Ibid p. 23.
30. Ibid p. 22.
31. Ibid p. 74.

32. Ibid p. 77.
33. Testimonial from a Later Davidian worker's conversation with H.M.S. Richards, Sr..
34. "Signs of the Times," Review and Herald Publishing Assn., January 30, 1934, p. 6.
36. VT Houteff, "The White-House Recruiter," Universal Publishing Assn., pp. 53-55.
37. Ibid p. 72.

Notes to Chapter 5

1. 1 Kings 18:19-40 (KJV).
2. VT Houteff, "The Symbolic Code," Universal Publishing Assn.vol.1 #14 p.5.
3. Issues: "The Seventh-day Adventists and Certain Private Ministries North American Division, p. 148.
4. W.L. Ferry and Virginia Stocker, petitioners versus The General Conference Corp. of S.D.A. respondent brief.
5. VT Houteff, "Tract No. 13," Universal Publishing Assn. pp. 44, 45
6. V:T: Houteff, "Timely Greetings, Universal publishing Assn., vol. 1 #17 p. 5.
7. VT Houteff, "Jezreel Letters," Universal Publishing Assn.,
8. "Timely Greetings," vol. 1 p. 19.
9. Chris Witchcraft, Waco Tribune-Herald February 27, 1955.
10. Testimonials of pioneers, workers, and friends.
11. "The Symbolic Code," vol. 1 #2 p. 2.
12. "The Symbolic Code," vol. 1 #10 pp. 3, 4.
13. "The Symbolic Code," vol. 1 #11, 12 p. 1.
14. "The Symbolic Code," vol. 10 #3, 4 pp. 27, 28.
15. "The Symbolic Code," vol. 1 #11, 12 P· 2·
16. "The Symbolic Code," vol. 1 #14 p. 1.
19. "Mt. Carmel Training Center Catalog-Syllabus, Rules Manual, 1942, p. 10.
20. "The Symbolic Code," vol. 5 #6-12 pp. 2, 3.
21. PP·V.T. 5-9. Houteff, "The Answerer," Universal Publishing Assn. bk. 5

Notes to Chapter 6

1. VT Houteff, "The Answerer, Universal Publishing Assn. bk. 5 pp. 82, 83.

2. VT Houteff, "Timely Greetings, Universal Publishing Assn. vol. 2, #38 pp. 13-19.

3. "Mt. Carmel Training Center Catalog-Syllabus and Rules Manual, p. 18.

4. "The Answerer," bk. 5 p. 5.

5. "Mt. Carmel Training Center Catalog-Syllabus and Rules Manual, pp.22, 23.

6. VT Houteff, "The Symbolic Code," vol. 2 #12, p. 8.

7. Testimonies, Memoirs of earlier workers and friends

8. 1 Samuel 17:1-58 (KJV).

9. Timely Greetings," vol. 2 #10 pp. 17, 18.

10. "The Symbolic Code, "vol. 8 #1-12 p. 24.

11. "The Symbolic Code," vol. 3 #2 p. 3.

12. "The Symbolic Code," vol. 9 #1-12 p. 24.

13. "The Leviticus of Davidian Seventh-day Adventists," (preface) P· L

14. "Fundamental Beliefs of Davidian Seventh-day Adventists," pp. 16-3

15. "The Symbolic Code," vol. 4 #1-3 pp. 4, 5.

16. "Timely Greetings," vol. 2 #35 p. 24.

17. E.G. White, "Counsels to Writers and Editors," Southern Publishing Assn., pp. 35, 37.

18. "Timely Greetings," vol. 1 #13 p. 6.

19. "The Answerer," bk. 1 p. 46.

20. "The Answerer," bk. 5 p. 55.

21. Ibid pp. 28, 29.

22. "Timely Greetings," vol. 2 #44 p. 30.

23. "The History and Teachings of 'The Shepherd's Rod' The Committee on Defense of the General Conference of S.D.A., October 1955, pp.20, 21.

24. Exodus 4:14 (KJV).

25. Leviticus 8:1-13 (KJV).

26. Exodus 15:20-21 (KJV).

27. "The Symbolic Code," vol. 3 #5 p. 7.

28. VT Houteff, "The Entering Wedge, Universal Publishing Assn., reply letter, October 12, 1952, pp. 1-3.

29. "The Symbolic Code," vol. 3 #5 pp. 5, 6.

30. "The Answerer," bk. 2 pp. 55, 56.

Notes to Chapter 7

1. VT Houteff, "Timely Greetings, Universal Publishing Assn., vol. 1 #14 pp. 16, 17.
2. VT Houteff, "The Answerer, Universal Publishing Assn., bk. 1 p. 94.
3. VT Houteff, "The Symbolic Code., Universal Publishing Assn., vol. 13 #3, 4 pp. 6, 7.
4. Ibid p. 10.
5. "The Symbolic Code," vol. 12 #1 p. 6.
6. VT Houteff, "Tract No. 14," Universal Publishing Assn., p. 24.
7. "The Symbolic Code," vol. 12 #1 p. 24.
8. "Tract No. 14," (supplement), p. 4.
9. "Timely Greetings," vol. 1 #4 p. 23.
10. "Timely Greetings," vol. 2 #41, pp. 16-20.
11. "Timely Greetings," vol. 1 #19 p. 3.
12. "Timely Greetings," vol. 1 #20 p. 11
13. "Timely Greetings," vol. 1 #22 pp. 24-26.
14. "Timely Greetings, " vol. 1 #12 p. 24.
15. "Tract No. 12," pp. 54, 55.
16. "Timely Greetings," vol. 2 #36, p. 7.
17. "Timely Greetings, " vol. 2 #18 p. 20.
18. "Timely Greetings," vol. 2 #17 p. 13.
19. "You Can Trust the Communists (to be Communists)," Dr. Fred Swartz
20. Anatoli Golitsyn, "New Lies for Old," 1984.
21. E.G. White, Manuscript Releases," E.G. White Estate, Wash. D.C., vol. 1 p.260
22. E.G. White, "Testimonies for the Church," Pacific Press Publishing Assn., vol. 5 p. 211.
23. "Tract No. 9," pp. 25, 26.
24. "Encyclopedia Britanica," 1992 edition, vol. 10, p. 942.
25. Revelation 21 (KJV)
26. "Timely Greetings," vol. 1 #40 p. 22.
27. Revelation 7:4 (KJV)
28. "Timely Greetings," vol. 1 #4 pp. 17, 18.
29. E.G. White, "Testimonies to Ministers and Gospel Workers," Pacific: Press Publishing Assn., p. 300.

Notes to Chapter 8

1. VT Houteff, "The White House Recruiter, Universal Publishing Assn., p. 33.
2. VT Houteff, "Timely Greetings," Universal Publishing Assn., vol. 1 #5 p. 18.
3. "Timely Greetings," vol. 7 #8 p. 9.
4. VT Houteff, "The Symbolic Code," Universal Publishing Assn., vol. 11 #2 pp. 10, 11.
5. Testimonials of pioneers workers, and friends.
6. "Timely Greetings," vol. 2 #46 pp. 48, 49.
7. VT Houteff, "Jezreel Letters," Universal Publishing Assn., #9 p. 3.
8. "The Symbolic Code," vol. 10 #1 p. 3.
9. "The Symbolic Code," vol. 10 #2 p. 11.
10. See #8 p. 6.
11. "The Symbolic Code," vol. 11 #12 pp. 30,31.
12. "The Symbolic Code," vol. 10 #3,4 pp. 16, 17, Feb. 1955.
13. "The Symbolic Code," vol. 11#8 p. 22.
14. Numbers 14:33, 34 (KJV).
15. Ezra 4:6 (KJV).
16. E.G. White, "The Great Controversy," Pacific Press Publishing Assn., p. 324.
17. VT Houteff, "Tract No. 5," Universal Publishing Assn., pp. 112-114.
18. Letter from the general office, "What Davidians are Expecting After April, 22, [1959], spring 1959 (no specific date).
19. VT Houteff. "The Answerer." Universal Publishing Assn.,
20. "History and Teachings of The Shepherd's Rod'" The Committee on Defense Literature of the General Conference of SDA, Oct. 1955 pp.52-60.
21. Letter from Mrs. VT Houteff, June 23, 1959, pp. 1-2.
22. "The Symbolic Code," vol. 14 #6 pp. 27-28, Feb. 1959.
23. Thomas Turner, Dallas Morning News, April, 1959.
24. Waco News Tribune, April 21, 1959.
25. Ibid, April 22, 1959.
26. Ibid, May 2, 1959.
27. Ray Bell, Waco Tribune-Herald, May 3, 1959

Notes to Chapter 9

1. Idries Shah, "Caravan of Dreams," Penguin Books, 1968, p. 137.
2. "Committee for Waco Justice," p. 8
3. Ibid p. 15.
4. Gustav Nieguhr and Pierre Thomas, April 25, 1993, A 20.
5. "Cult Kid Discipline Cough, But Wasn't Abuse, Says Doctor, Washington Times, May 6, 1993.
6. Paul H. Blackman report, "Affidavit to Kill, Institute for Legislative Action, National Rifle Assn. p. 33.
7. Michael Decourcy Hinds, April 20, 1993, A 20.
8. Joseph L. Galloway, "IJ.S. News and World Report," October 4, 1993 pp.73,75.
9. "America," editorial, May 22, 1993.
10. VT Houteff, "Timely Greetings, Universal Publishing Assn., vol. 1 #50 pp.23, 24.
11. "Funk and Wagnalls, Comprehensive International Dictionary of the English Language, deluxe ed., 1471-1982.
12. A.T. Jones "Civil Government and Religion" American Sentinel, 1989
13. Matthew 5:39 (KJV).
14. Revelation 13:10 (KJV).
15. E.G. White, "Testimonies for the Church," Pacific Press Publishing Assn., vol. 9 p. 260.
16. "Caravan of Dreams," p. 155.
17. "Timely Greetings," vol. 2 #45 pp. 6-8.

Notes to Chapter 10

1. VT Houteff, "Timely Greetings," Universal Publishing Assn., vol. 1 #31 p. 8.
2. Testimonials of workers and pioneers
3. 2 Corinthians 4:6, 8, 9 (KJV)

Please Note: All notes entitled "Testimonials of pioneers, workers and friends," or similar titles, represent testimonies acquired from several persons whom did not wish to be identified.
Such sources were either former members and/or workers, or pioneers, members, or workers who still embrace the Davidian SDA teachings.

Author

ABOUT THE AUTHOR

Dr. A. Anthony Hibbert has had considerable personal knowledge and encounters with Branch believers, he has studied their beliefs, history and doctrines. He has published numerous articles about the Davidian Seventh-day Adventists.

As an authority, he was called upon as an expert witness in depositions relating to Davidian S.D.A's.

He has traveled extensively in the US, Canada, Europe, Africa and the West Indies lecturing on the teachings of Davidians. He has been interviewed by the New York Times and the Times Herald Record newspapers. Dr. Hibbert has also appeared as a guest on numerous radio and television programs.

He is currently the Chairman/Vice-President, Ordained Minister and Bible Instructor in the General Association of Davidian Seventh-day Adventist.